THE RIGHT WAY TO KNIT

A Manual for Basic Knitting

By

EVELYN STILES STEWART

Illustrations by **Frederick Cross**

Photography by **Edward G. Tracy**

CONTENTS

	Page
Abbreviations, Knitting	5
Symbols and Definitions, Knitting	5–6
Beginner's Work Sheet	6
Yarn and Needles	7
Good Materials and Good Tools	7
Preparing Your Yarn for Knitting	7
Labels	8
Dye Lots	8
Balling Yarn	9
How to Make a Slip Loop	10
Casting on Stitches	12
Hands and Fingers	12
Method No. 1 Casting on	12
Preparations to Knitting	13
Front and Back of Work	13
Right or Left of a Stitch	13
Where to Insert Needle for Knit Stitch	13
Knitting Position of Body and Hands	14
How to Hold Needles	14
How to Hold Both Needles with Left Hand	14
How to Hold Yarn with Right Hand	15
Knitting	16
The Knit Stitch	16
Steps 1-2-3-4 Knit	16
Row	18
Turning at Ends of Rows	18
Garter Stitch	18
How to Recognize a Knit Stitch	18
Some Knit Tips for Knitting Problems	19
Gaining Extra Stitches at Beginning of Knit Rows	19
Feeding New Stitches with Left Hand	20
Adjusting Stitches on Needles	20
Rhythm in Knitting	20
Losing Needle Out of Work at Beginning of Rows	21
Right Needle in Right Hand when Resuming Knitting	21
Short Rows	21
Tension	21
The Individual's Tension	22
Effects of your Physical and Nervous System on Your Knitting	22
Gauge	22
Stitches Per Inch	23
Rows Per Inch	23
Adjustment to Get Gauge	23
Some Habits that Cause:	24
Too Tight Knitting	24
Too Loose Knitting	25
A Second Way to Hold Yarn	25
Left-Handed Knitters	25
Mistakes and Extra Stitches	26
How to Correct Mistakes	26
How to Correct Dropped Stitches	28
Purl Stitch	30
Steps 1-2-3-4 Purl	30
If Purl Stitches are Looser Than Knit Stitches	31
Gaining Extra Stitches at Beginning of Purl Rows	31
Stockinette Stitch	32
Reverse Stockinette	32
Unevenness of Rows and Stitches	32
Edges of Rows — Basic Don'ts	33
Joining Yarns	33
How Much Yarn to Work One Row?	34
Where to Join Yarns?	34
How to Join Yarns?	34
Knots	35
Why Be Particular?	35
Ribbing	36
K 2, P 2	36
Making Ribbing Easy	37
K 3, P 3	37
K 1, P 1	38
Slip Stitch	38
Purlwise	38
Knitwise	38
For Turning Edge	39
Binding Off	39
Method No. 1 Knitwise and Purlwise	39
Last Loop on Needle When Binding Off Too Tightly	40
Method No. 2	40

	Page
Increases	41
Method No. 1 — Knitwise	41
Method No. 1 — Purlwise	41
Method No. 2 — Picking Up Stitch	42
Method No. 3 — Knitwise	42
Method No. 3 — Purlwise	43
Method No. 4 — Cast on Stitches on Edge	43
Method No. 5 — Increases by Yarn Over (YO)	43
Yarn Overs	43
The Secret of Making Yarn Overs	43
Basic YO Combinations	43
K 1, YO, K 1	43
K 1, YO, P 1	44
P 1, YO, P 1	44
P 1, YO, K 1	44
Method No. 6 — "English" Make One	44
Some Uses for YO's	45
Decreases	45
Working Stitches Together	45
Pass Slip Stitch Over or Slip, Knit and Pass	45
Matching Decreases	46
Decrease to Match K 2 tog.	47
Decrease to Match S1 1, K 1, PSSO	47
Knitting Continental Fashion	48
Casting on	48
With Left Side of Loop on Front of Needle	48
With Right Side of Loop on Front of Needle	48
Learning to Read Instructions	48
Errors in Patterns	49
Other Methods of Casting On	50
Method No. 1 — Purlwise	50
Method No. 2 — Knitwise	50
Method No. 3 — Knitwise	51
Method No. 3 — Purlwise	51
Method No. 3 — In Pattern	52
Knitting Needles and Accessories	52
Row Counter, Stitch Holders and Markers, and Sewing Needles	52–53
How to Change Needles	54
Preparing Yarns for Reknitting	54
Some Basic Pattern Stitches	55
Seed Stitch	55

	Page
Double Seed Stitch	56
Cable Stitch and Variations	57
Basic Ways to Write Cable Pattern	58
Right Twist	59
Left Twist	60
Fabric Stitch and Variation	60
Quaker Rib	61
Popcorn Stitch	61
Fisherman's Rib	61
Some Characteristics of Pattern Stitches	62
Knitting	63
Scarfs	63
Garter Stitch	63
Stockinette with Garter Borders	63
Broken Rib with Fringe	64
Cable with Garter Borders	64
Popcorn with Garter Borders	64
Fancy Pattern with Garter Borders	65
How To Design Your Own Scarf	65
Man's Contour Scarf	66
Baby Blankets	67
Stockinette with Garter Borders	67
Strips of Ribbing and Stockinette with Garter Borders	67
Block Pattern with Garter Stitch Borders	67
Center Block and Borders in Seed Stitch	68
Double Cable with Garter Borders	68
Mock Cable with Fringe Trim	69
Feather and Fan with Garter Borders	69
Deep Toboggan	69
Cable Earwarmer	70
TV or Bed Slippers	71
Ski Headband	71
"Ball" Hat	72
Mittens (two needles)	72
How To Make	
Fringe	73
Tassels	73
Pom Pons	74
Cord	74
Advice From and To Knitters	75
Knitting Record Sheet	76

Hello!

So you're going to learn to knit! Good! Let's learn "THE RIGHT WAY".

You will be so proud of your knitting and it's such great fun doing it! It is very relaxing and a great satisfaction creating your own garments.

You will find today's knitting, very FASHIONABLE, PRACTICAL, NECESSARY IN A SMART WARDROBE AND YES, — SO QUICK AND EASY TO DO!

Learning to knit "THE RIGHT WAY" COSTS VERY LITTLE. Tools and materials needed are one pair of needles and one skein of knitting worsted.

Since few knitters have the opportunity for professional instruction, I have written step-by-step instructions on how to learn the basic stitches. This method, which has been developed over many years and used by hundreds of knitters, TEACHES YOU TO KNIT. At the same time, you are told "WHY?" you should do your work in this particular fashion. These detailed explanations will ELIMINATE OR SOLVE THE PROBLEMS MOST KNITTERS HAVE. When you know "HOW?" and "WHY?", knitting is easy and quick to do.

You will learn KNITTING LANGUAGE, — its terms, definitions, symbols and abbreviations.

You will learn to READ PATTERNS.

You will learn many KNIT TIPS, rules and important explanations not written, taught or included in regular pattern books.

You will knit a small item of your choice, like an earwarmer, scarf, blanket for baby, pair of mittens, TV slippers, etc.

By the time you have done all this, I guarantee that you will be most anxious to start your first sweater and if you are like most new knitters, you will have planned the next four or five items you want to make.

FOR QUICK LEARNING TO KNIT, FOLLOW THE PICTURES AND READ ONLY THIS LARGE PRINT. THIS SIZE PRINT WILL BE USED FOR INSTRUCTIONS, ACTUAL WORK WITH YARN AND NEEDLES, KNIT TIPS AND "MUST" READING.

Children will surprise you learning to knit using ONLY the pictures.

This "smaller size print" is for the person who wishes more information for expert knitting, solving your knitting problems and achieving our knitting goal . . .

HAND MADE WITH THE PROFESSIONAL LOOK!

Using "THE RIGHT WAY TO KNIT" you will be delighted with the quality of your work and the beauty of your knitting.

You are about to gain a life-long friend and companion in the ART OF HAND KNITTING. It has brought great pleasure, comfort, and happiness to many and I hope it will do the same for you.

Knittingly yours,

Evelyn Stiles Stewart

KNITTING ABBREVIATIONS

beg	beginning
cc	contrast color
dec	decrease
dp	double-pointed
in	inch
inc	increase
incl	inclusive
ins	inches
k	knit
mc	main color
p	purl
pat	pattern
psso	pass slip stitch over
rpt or rep	repeat
rnd	round
skp	slip, knit and pass
sl	slip
sl st	slip stitch
ss	stockinette stitch
sts	stitches
st st	stockinette stitch
tog	together
yo	yarn over

SYMBOLS AND DEFINITIONS

*	asterick or star
* to *	Instructions between *'s are going to be repeated. First, work from * to *. Then continue repeating between *'s as many times as indicated after second *.
**	Double asterick or star is used in same manner as single *. This ** to **is often used to indicate a repeated section within * to *.
† to †	Dagger, used in same manner as *. This is used more often in crocheting.
Blocking	Steaming or pressing knits into shape.
( ) [ ]	Parentheses or brackets are used:

    1. In listing sizes of garments, as: Size 12 (14-16-18).

    2. To indicate sections that are to be repeated a given number of times as: (YO, K1) 6 times.

    3. To contain explanations as in Cable Earwarmer on Page 70.

"Ending with a knit or purl row"	The row has been worked.
Garment	Any knitted item to be worn.
Gauge	The number of stitches per inch horizontally and the number of rows per inch vertically.
Item	Object being made.
K 1	Knit one stitch.
K 2 tog.	Knit two stitches together.
Knitwise	Work like a knit stitch.
Loop	A stitch on a needle.
Motif	A group of stitches that makes a design or pattern.
Multiple	The number of stitches that are necessary to make a motif or design.

Multiple plus a given number of stitches	The plus number of stitches are necessary to center the motifs or designs or to allow enough stitches to make pattern work.	
Piece	Any sized section of knitting, finished or unfinished.	
Ply	Means strand or thread, as knitting worsted is a 4 ply yarn (four threads).	
P 1	Purl one stitch.	
P 2 tog.	Purl two stitches together.	
Purlwise	Work like purling.	
Swatch	A test piece or a small knitted sample of the pattern stitch.	
Tension	The tightness yarn is held when knitting.	
Test Piece	A swatch made with the yarn and needles used in the body section of a garment to learn pattern and check stitch gauge.	
Thread	Yarn or materials for knitting.	
Turn	Reverse work so needles are in opposite hands, even if this is in the middle of a row.	
Work	Continue in established pattern.	
Work even	Continue in established pattern without increasing or decreasing.	

BEGINNER'S WORK SHEET

	DATE STARTED	DATE LEARNED
1. Preparing wool for work		
2. Casting on Method No. 1		
3. Knit Stitch (Garter Stitch)		
4. Purl Stitch		
5. Stockinette Stitch		
6. Ribbing		
K 2, P 2		
K 3, P 3		
K 1, P 1		
7. Seed Stitch		
8. Decreasing		
9. Increasing Method No. 1		
10. Binding off Method No. 1		
11. Casting on Method No. 3		
12. Slip Stitch		
13. Cable Stitch		
14. Double Seed Stitch		
15.		
16.		
17.		
18.		

YARN AND NEEDLES

TO BEGIN YOUR KNITTING, YOU WILL NEED YARN AND NEEDLES. I SUGGEST THAT YOU PURCHASE ONE 4 OZ. SKEIN ALL WOOL KNITTING WORSTED IN A MEDIUM OR LIGHT SHADE OF COLOR. THIS WILL BE SUFFICIENT FOR LEARNING STITCHES AND KNITTING ONE SMALL ITEM. 1

1

I recommend using this all wool 4-ply yarn because it is a size easy to handle, easy to see, works up quickly, and has natural elasticity.

I RECOMMEND THAT YOU ALSO PURCHASE ONE PAIR NO. 8 STRAIGHT METAL KNITTING NEEDLES — 14" LONG, FOR KNITTING THIS YARN. 2

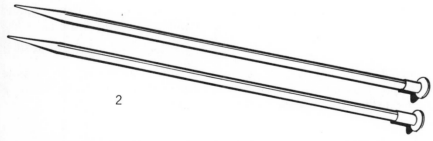

2

Size No. 8 needles are probably used more than any other size at this time, but the needles can be Size 9 or 10, — Size 10 being an excellent one for children. With care, metal needles will last many years. The 14" length gives you needles for as few or as many stitches as may be needed for regular flat knitting.

GOOD MATERIALS AND GOOD TOOLS MAKE THE EXCELLENT GARMENT

It is important that you work with the best quality yarns and tools you can secure and afford. Your time and energy deserve only the best material for the finest knits. These materials are found in yarn shops and art needlework departments, which will have a wide selection of yarns, needles, accessories, up-to-date pattern books, services and personnel to help you in selection of material. Many shops and stores have a knitting teacher, usually called an "instructress".

Although I prefer to use the knitting worsted and No. 8 needles for teaching, it is quite possible to learn on other yarns, thread and materials — even with such crude materials as sticks and string. In fact, the first knitting was probably done by shepherds using raw wool, from the sheep they tended, and small sticks for needles.

PREPARING YOUR YARN FOR KNITTING

Yarn is prepared in skeins, hanks, balls, pull-skeins and sometimes cones (for machine knitting). 3 Pull-skeins and balls of yarn are ready to use and yarn is pulled from the center.

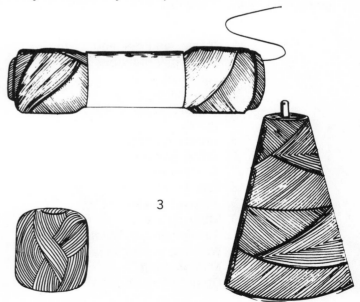

3

Knitting worsted usually comes in skeins or hanks. Yarn has been wound into a circle on a large reel, tied, folded and covered with a paper label. This means that the yarn must be wound into a ball or pull-skein before hand knitting. These skeins are usually prepared in 2 oz. or 4 oz. skeins — the 4 oz. skeins consisting of two 2 oz. skeins.

LABELS

REMOVE THE PAPER LABEL FROM THE YARN. READ IT. KEEP ALL LABELS UNTIL THE GARMENT IS FINISHED.

Many times a knitter decides to alter a pattern, makes a garment longer or larger, or perhaps loses part of the yarn, so additional yarn may need to be purchased. The most important information on the label is the color number and the dye lot number.

Information put on most labels:

1. Name, address and country of manufacturer
2. Name of yarn
3. Content of yarn
4. Weight, in ounces or grams
5. Article number
6. Color number
7. Color name
8. Dye lot number
9. Amount of yardage
10. Stitch gauge
11. Recommended needle size
12. Washing instructions
13. Mothproofing
14. Other information

DYE LOTS

YARNS ARE DYED IN CERTAIN QUANTITIES CALLED "LOTS". EACH LOT HAS A NUMBER. DIFFERENT LOTS OF THE SAME COLOR MAY VARY IN SHADE. THEREFORE, IT IS IMPORTANT THAT YOU PURCHASE ENOUGH YARN OF ONE DYE LOT TO FINISH ONE ENTIRE GARMENT.

Two different dye lots of the same color should not be in the same piece of knitting, for ninety-nine times out of a hundred, the difference in shade will show, especially on plain knitting, making the knit unsatisfactory.

However, if in order to finish a garment, usually a sleeve, two dye lots must be used, try to secure a shade that matches very closely and make the entire piece of one dye lot only. After garment is assembled, the variance in shade seldom shows.

If you must use a lot that does not match, try alternating two rows of new lot and two rows of old lot for several rows.

A "no dye lot" yarn is guaranteed to match in the same color and shade of any lot. Since these yarns take special handling and processing, they are expensive to manufacture and will cost a few cents more per skein.

A "matched dye lot" is one that is dyed as closely as possible to previous lots of the same color but variance in shade makes a dye lot number necessary for some colors.

It is well to do as your yarn sales personnel will suggest — buy all of your yarn at one time, of one dye lot, for one knitted garment. However, sales personnel are human and even using great care, can make errors in checking dye lots. It is wise for YOU to check that all skeins have the same dye lot number before breaking open any skeins.

Should you buy in excess of the quantity necessary for your knitting, most yarn shops and art needlework departments will accept returns of full skeins that are from open stock. Some stores do not allow return of yarn.

CHECK WITH YOUR STORE TO SEE IF YOU MAY RETURN FULL SKEINS OF LEFT-OVER YARN AND IF THERE IS ANY LIMITATION OF TIME. DO NOT EXPECT TO RETURN YARNS FROM KITS, SPECIAL ORDERS, SPECIAL SALES OR CLOSE-OUT YARNS.

When you have finished a garment, jot down on the "Knitting Record Sheet", Page 76, the number of labels, kind of yarn and amount of yardage used. This will be a guide for future purchases of the same yarn.

If you have a favorite pattern, many times you will be able to substitute other yarns and make several very different looking garments with the unlimited variety in color and texture available today.

Since yarn is sold by weight, you may need to purchase more or fewer balls of yarn than pattern calls for in order to get sufficient yardage when substituting comparable yarns.

For example: A 2 oz. skein of knitting worsted may contain from 133 to 140 yards. Some other 2 oz. skeins, which knit to the same gauge, vary greatly and may contain 170, 96, 86, or 120 yards.

THE AMOUNT OF YARDAGE IN EACH SKEIN MUST BE KNOWN TO ASSURE PROPER SUBSTITUTION OF YARNS. REGARDLESS OF HOW MANY GRAMS OR OUNCES PATTERN CALLS FOR, A SUFFICIENT NUMBER OF YARDS OF YARN MUST BE SECURED FOR KNITTING A GARMENT.

BALLING YARN

SEPARATE THE TWO SECTIONS OF THE 4 OZ. SKEIN OF KNITTING WORSTED AND PREPARE YARN FOR KNITTING, USING ONE OF THE FOLLOWING METHODS:

1. FOR THE BEGINNER, PLACE THE YARN OVER THE BACK OF A STRAIGHT CHAIR OR ON A YARN SPINDLE OR HAVE SOMEONE HOLD IT FOR YOU. 4

4

WIND THE YARN INTO A LOOSE SOFT BALL. YARN MUST NEVER BE WOUND TIGHTLY SINCE THIS "STRINGS" THE YARN AND THE GARMENT WILL HAVE NO ELASTICITY OR "SPRING".

AN EASY WAY TO WIND YARN IS TO WRAP YARN OVER TWO OR THREE FINGERS SEVERAL TIMES, REMOVE FINGERS, AND ALWAYS TURNING THE BALL, REPEAT UNTIL COMPLETELY WOUND. 5

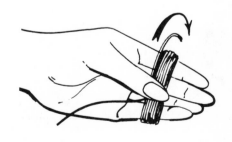 

5

IN THIS INSTANCE, YARN WILL BE USED FROM OUTSIDE OF THE BALL.

2. Make a pull-skein by hand as follows: Putting end of yarn toward floor and in palm of hand, lay yarn back and forth as for making a ribbon bow for trimming. Wrap yarn several times around the center thickness of the bow section, leaving first end loose to be pulled later. Wind balance of yarn over this center section and into ball. Tuck in end on outside of ball. Pull beginning end of yarn from center for knitting.

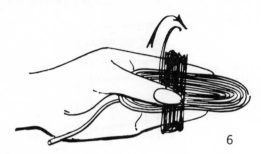

6

3. Make a pull-skein on a pencil or stick as follows: Leaving end of yarn extending over end of pencil, wrap yarn in a figure eight motion around pencil. Tuck in end of yarn on outside and pull out pencil. Pull first end of yarn from center or pull skein.

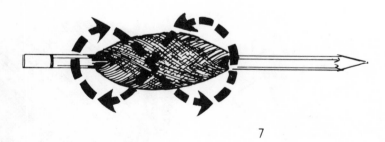

7

4. Wind on manual or electric yarn winder. Manual winders can be purchased for the individual knitter and many shops have electric winders as a free service for their knitters.

HOW TO MAKE A SLIP LOOP
KNITTING IS SIMPLY BRINGING A LOOP OF YARN THROUGH ANOTHER LOOP OF YARN. 8

We know it is very easy to bring a loop through a loop but since we can't make the correct size loops with our fingers, we learn to use tools called "needles and knitting accessories". Our hands and tools are actually going to work like a little machine. With this method of learning to knit, this finger machine is a very simple one, working in the QUICKEST, EASIEST WAY FOR THE BEST RESULTS. As your hands and needles coordinate to handle the tools and make the stitches, you will be surprised how much fun it is and the real pleasure you get in smooth, even knitting, quickly done.

8

TO BEGIN OUR KNITTING, WE MUST HAVE LOOPS ON THE NEEDLE. THE PROCESS OF PUTTING THESE LOOPS ON THE NEEDLE IS CALLED "CASTING ON".

TO CAST ON STITCHES OR LOOPS, WE START WITH A SLIP LOOP.

STEP 1 SLIP LOOP

PLACE END FROM BALL OF YARN LEFT HAND. 9

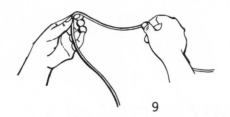

9

STEP 2 SLIP LOOP

MAKE A CIRCLE OF YARN OVER THE LEFT HAND, DROPPING THE YARN TO BACK. 10

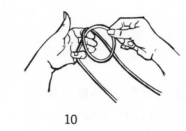

10

STEP 3 SLIP LOOP

REACH THROUGH THE CIRCLE AND PULL YARN THROUGH FROM BACK TO FRONT. 11

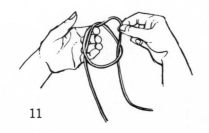

11

STEP 4 SLIP LOOP

PUT LOOP IN LEFT HAND AND WITH RIGHT HAND PICK UP A NEEDLE AND INSERT IN CENTER OF THIS LOOP. 12

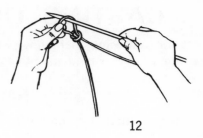

12

STEP 5 SLIP LOOP

PULL BOTH PIECES OF YARN UNTIL A KNOT IS MADE. 13

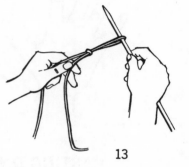

13

STEP 6 SLIP LOOP

PULL YARN ATTACHED TO BALL AND KNOT WILL SLIDE UP UNDERNEATH NEEDLE. 14

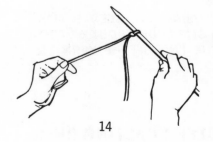

14

YOU HAVE MADE A SLIP LOOP. PRACTICE SEVERAL TIMES.

THIS CAST-ON LOOP IS USED TO BEGIN ALL TYPES OF CASTING ON AND IS COUNTED AS THE FIRST LOOP OR STITCH.

CASTING ON STITCHES

For easy remembering, we will number the various methods of casting on. Other methods of casting on begin on Page 50.

HANDS

For knitting, we number the fingers from the thumb out, as in 15.

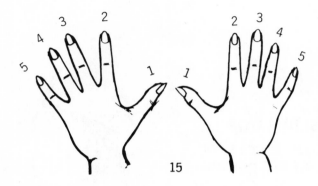

CASTING ON METHOD NO. 1

USING ONE NEEDLE, MAKE A SLIP LOOP ABOUT 6" FROM THE END OF THE YARN 16

STEP 1 CASTING ON 16

PUT NEEDLE IN RIGHT HAND. TAKE YARN ATTACHED TO BALL IN LEFT HAND, PLACING SECOND OR INDEX FINGER OF LEFT HAND ON TOP OF YARN.

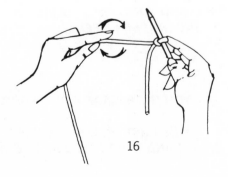

STEP 2 CASTING ON 17

MAKE A LOOP ON LEFT HAND INDEX FINGER BY GOING DOWN AND UNDER YARN.

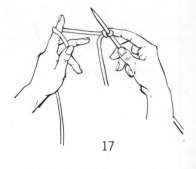

STEP 3 CASTING ON 18

INSERT NEEDLE AT LEFT FRONT SIDE OF LOOP, THROUGH LOOP AND ON TOP OF FINGER.

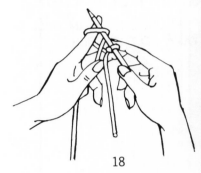

STEP 4 CASTING ON 19

SLIP YARN OFF FINGER ONTO NEEDLE AND PULL YARN UNTIL LOOP FITS NEEDLE.

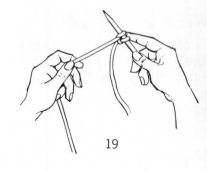

REPEAT STEPS 1 - 2 - 3 - 4 CASTING ON UNTIL 24 LOOPS ARE ON NEEDLE. 20

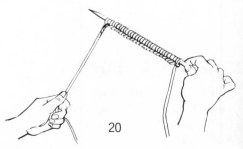

Yarn should be pulled up, not too tight nor too loose. Yarn is "bouncy" and will shape to the needle nicely.

ANYTIME YOU ARE CASTING ON AND THE STITCHES ARE NOT PUT ON SMOOTHLY AND EVENLY, PULL THEM OFF AND CAST ON AGAIN. IT IS ALMOST IMPOSSIBLE TO CORRECT CAST-ON ROW SATISFACTORILY AFTER IT IS ONCE KNITTED.

This Method No. 1 is useful for casting on stitches by beginning knitters, for underarm shaping as for dolman sleeves, for top edges of buttonholes and for increasing on side edges with some bulky yarns.

WE USE 24 STITCHES FOR LEARNING SINCE WE NEED A NUMBER DIVISIBLE BY 2, 3 OR 4 FOR DIFFERENT PATTERN STITCHES.

PREPARING TO KNIT
FRONT AND BACK OF WORK

THE SIDE OF THE NEEDLES CLOSEST TO YOU AND FACING YOU IS CALLED THE FRONT OF THE NEEDLES OR THE FRONT OF THE WORK. THE OPPOSITE SIDE, YOU CANNOT SEE, IS CALLED THE BACK OF THE NEEDLES OR THE BACK OF THE WORK. 21

This applies only to the actual knitting of the piece and does not mean the right side or wrong side of the knitted garment.

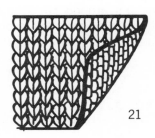

21

THE RIGHT OR LEFT OF A STITCH 22

LOOKING NOW AT THE FRONT OF THE NEEDLE, ANYTHING TO THE RIGHT OF THIS FIRST LOOP IS CALLED ON THE RIGHT SIDE OF THE STITCH AND ANYTHING TO THE LEFT OF THE FIRST LOOP IS CALLED ON THE LEFT SIDE OF THE STITCH.

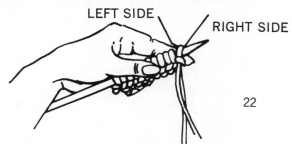

LEFT SIDE   RIGHT SIDE

22

WHERE TO INSERT NEEDLE FOR THE KNIT STITCH

SO YOU MAY EASILY SEE THE CENTER OF THE LOOP LAYING FLAT, AND WHERE YOU WILL BRING THE YARN THROUGH TO MAKE THE NEW KNIT STITCH, PULL UP OR LOOSEN THE FIRST LOOP A LITTLE. 23

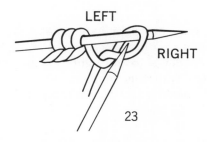

LEFT

RIGHT

23

YOU WILL NOTICE THAT THE LOOPS ON THE NEEDLE LEAN A LITTLE TO THE RIGHT. WE WILL ALWAYS HAVE THE RIGHT SIDE OF THE LOOP ON THE FRONT OF THE NEEDLE FOR THIS METHOD OF KNITTING. ALL LOOPS ON THE NEEDLE WILL LAY IN THE SAME DIRECTION. IF THEY ARE NOT, YOU HAVE MADE AN ERROR IN CASTING ON.

NOW PULL END OF YARN BACK IN PLACE SO FIRST STITCH IS EVEN WITH THE OTHERS AND READY TO KNIT.

KNITTING POSITION OF BODY AND HANDS

LIKE ANY OTHER ACTIVITY WHERE YOU WILL BE SITTING FOR ANY LENGTH OF TIME, USE A COMFORTABLE CHAIR THAT GIVES GOOD SUPPORT FOR GOOD POSTURE.

HOW TO HOLD NEEDLES

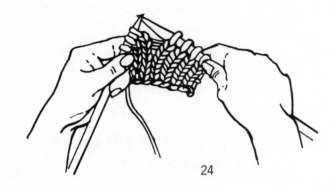

24

THE HANDS ARE PLACED ON TOP OF THE NEEDLES, WITH THE RIGHT HAND "THROWING" OR WRAPPING THE YARN. THIS IS THE "ENGLISH" FASHION OF HOLDING YARN AND NEEDLES. 24

Many knitters hold the right hand needle like a pencil, with the thumb under right needle at all times. I do not like this method because there is a tendency to knit tight with this method. Although there is less motion with this method, when knitted piece gets larger and thicker, there is just too much knitting wadded under the hand.

For Continental method of holding yarn in left hand, see Page 48.

FOR EFFICIENT MOTIONS, THE FINGERS ON THE RIGHT HAND ARE PLACED ABOUT 3-½" FROM THE TIP OF NEEDLE, AND LEFT HAND WILL BE ABOUT ½" BELOW THE BEGINNING OF GRADUATED TIP OF NEEDLE.

SINCE WE ARE USUALLY SEATED WHEN KNITTING, NEEDLES WILL REST ON LAP WITH ENDS OF NEEDLES POINTING TOWARD ELBOWS.

Do not wedge end of left needle in abdomen or leg. Do not hold needles one under each arm.

If the basic position of body and hands is not comfortable, each knitter should adjust their hand position for easy knitting, keeping hands close enough to ends of needles for efficient motions.

Children will normally place their hands further down on needle and usually make quite large motions, since their fingers are too small to do much individual finger work.

HOW TO HOLD BOTH NEEDLES WITH THE LEFT HAND

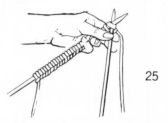

25

SLIP THE LEFT HAND THUMB, SECOND AND THIRD FINGERS STRAIGHT ACROSS AND BELOW FIRST LOOP ON RIGHT HAND NEEDLE. KEEPING THE "X" AT END OF NEEDLES, LET BOTH NEEDLES REST ON TIPS OF FINGERS. 25 THIS WILL FREE THE RIGHT HAND TO WRAP THE YARN AROUND THE POINT OF RIGHT NEEDLE.

Be sure that you are holding the needles BELOW the stitch on right hand needle. If fingers get in the way, yarn will be wrapped not only around needle but around parts of the fingers. Since it would be impossible to wrap fingers and needle exactly the same each time, this can cause loose, uneven knitting which will never be satisfactory.

It is advisable to be sure the second finger comes over flat to help hold both needles. Do not allow it to be caught between the needles or bent in a tight fashion, for it will become very tired after a short time.

The third finger is the "balancing" finger and will be very comfortable placed flat under the right needle.

HOW TO HOLD YARN WITH THE RIGHT HAND

FOR A NATURAL EASY WAY OF HOLDING THE YARN, YARN IS WOVEN OVER AND UNDER THE FINGERS ON RIGHT HAND SO YARN RESTS ON TOP OF THE SECOND AND FOURTH FINGERS.

YARN IS ALLOWED TO SLIDE EASILY THROUGH FINGERS WHEN NEEDED. THESE FINGERS DETERMINE HOW TIGHTLY THE YARN IS HELD.

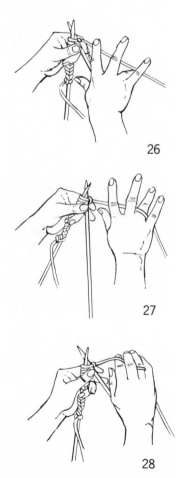

TO PICK UP YARN EASILY, ABOUT 6" FROM TIP OF NEEDLES, DROP THE FOURTH FINGER AND SLIDE IT UNDER YARN 26 *, AND PAST THE SECOND KNUCKLE ON FINGER* 27 *. YARN WILL NOT DROP OFF FOURTH FINGER IF IT IS KEPT BELOW THE SECOND KNUCKLE.*

26

27

PUT SECOND FINGER UNDER YARN AND REST YARN BETWEEN FIRST KNUCKLE AND BASE OF FINGERNAIL. 28

28

If yarn is difficult to pick up, be patient. ALWAYS hold yarn correctly in right hand. This will pay off with smooth, even knitting without fatigue.

If yarn is hard to pick up with the fourth finger, you might try the following: A little Brownie Girl Scout in one of my knitting classes solved the problem this way. "When I have trouble getting hold of the yarn, I just put the yarn between my knees and hold it tight until I get it on my fingers." This works fine and is very helpful, especially when teaching children.

PRACTICE MOTION: TO GET THE FEEL OF THE YARN, PRACTICE PICKING UP AND SLIDING THE HAND DOWN ALONG YARN. ALLOW THE YARN TO SLIDE THROUGH THE FINGERS SMOOTHLY AND EVENLY.

YOU WILL NOTICE THAT THE RIGHT HAND IS HELD EASILY, YARN IS WOVEN ON TOP OF CORRECT FINGERS AND FINGERS ARE SLIGHTLY CURVED, LIKE HOLDING A PENCIL, OR CUPPING A LITTLE WATER IN YOUR HAND.

This is a natural position and your hand will not get tired in this position when knitting. If you get any fatigue in the hands and arms, you are doing something wrong.

See Page 25 for a second way to hold yarn with the right hand.

KNITTING

IN THE ART OF KNITTING BY HAND, WE HAVE ONLY TWO BASIC STITCHES. ONE IS CALLED THE KNIT STITCH AND THE OTHER THE PURL STITCH. ALL KNITTING IS A COMBINATION OF KNIT AND PURL STITCHES. 29,30

THE KNIT STITCH IS SMOOTH..

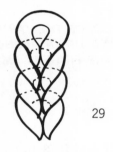

29

THE PURL STITCH IS ROUGH.

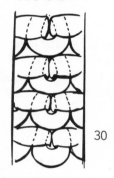

30

THE KNIT STITCH

STEP 1 KNIT

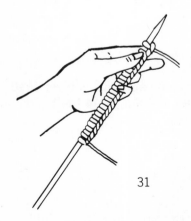

31

PUT NEEDLE WITH 24 CAST-ON LOOPS IN LEFT HAND. PLACE LEFT HAND ON TOP OF NEEDLE WITH THE THUMB AND INDEX FINGERS HOLDING BE-TWEEN THE FIRST AND SECOND LOOP.

31

PICKING UP OTHER NEEDLE WITH RIGHT HAND, PUT THIS NEEDLE INTO THE LEFT FRONT OF THE FIRST LOOP (THROUGH THE CENTER OF LOOP) AND CROSS NEEDLE UNDER AND TO BACK OF LEFT NEEDLE, MAKING AN "X" WITH THE NEEDLE POINTS. 32

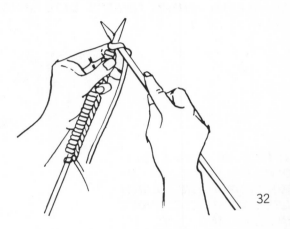

32

SLIDE THE LEFT HAND THUMB, SECOND AND THIRD FINGERS STRAIGHT ACROSS AND BELOW THIS FIRST LOOP ON RIGHT HAND NEEDLE. KEEPING THE "X" AT END OF THE NEEDLES, LET BOTH NEEDLES REST ON TIPS OF FINGERS. 33 THIS WILL FREE THE RIGHT HAND TO WRAP THE YARN AROUND THE POINT OF RIGHT NEEDLE.

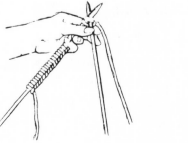

33

STEP 2 KNIT

WITH LEFT HAND HOLDING BOTH NEEDLES AND YARN WOVEN ON RIGHT HAND, WRAP YARN AROUND POINT OF RIGHT HAND NEEDLE AT BACK OF WORK, GOING IN DIRECTION TOWARD THE FLOOR, THEN TO THE LEFT (COUNTER-CLOCKWISE) AND AROUND NEEDLE. 34

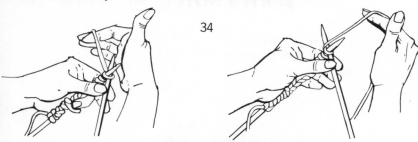

PULL YARN DOWN ALONG TOP OF RIGHT HAND NEEDLE UNTIL DRAWN STRAIGHT, RE-PLACING HAND ON TOP OF RIGHT NEEDLE WITH FINGERS COMFORTABLY ON AND AROUND NEEDLE. LEFT HAND FINGERS SLIP BACK TO LEFT NEEDLE. 35

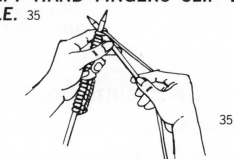

RIGHT NEEDLE RESTS ON INSIDE OF HAND BE-TWEEN THUMB AND ON ALL FINGERS. DO NOT ALLOW THE FOURTH AND FIFTH FINGERS TO CURL INTO PALM OF HAND, FOR HAND WILL GET TIRED IN THIS POSITION. IF LEFT HAND GETS TIRED, RELAX AND LET NEEDLES "REST" ON THE FINGERS.

STEP 3 KNIT

WITH RIGHT NEEDLE SCOOP UP AND PULL YARN THROUGH TO THE FRONT OF THE PIECE, PUSHING NEEDLE THROUGH TO THE "FAT" PART OF THE NEEDLE. THIS IS CALLED "SIZING THE STITCH" OR "SIZING THE NEEDLE". 36

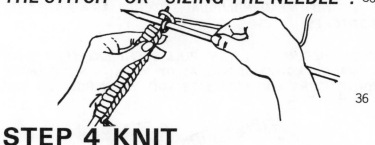

STEP 4 KNIT

NOW SLIP OR PULL OFF THE FIRST LOOP ON LEFT HAND NEEDLE OR WHAT IS CALLED THE "OLD STITCH". 37

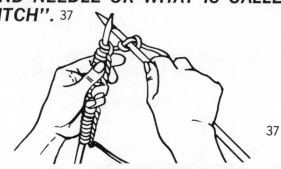

REPEAT THIS KNIT STITCH BY WORKING STEPS 1-2-3-4 KNIT, UNTIL ALL THE 24 LOOPS HAVE BEEN WORKED TO THE RIGHT HAND NEEDLE. 38

YOU HAVE KNITTED ONE ROW.

NOW, THERE! YOU DIDN'T THINK YOU COULD DO IT! THE KNIT STITCH IS VERY EASY TO DO. IT IS JUST GETTING ACCUS-TOMED TO USING THE TOOLS AND MATERIALS THAT TAKES A LITTLE TIME AND CAREFUL LEARNING.

R O W 38

WORKING EVERY STITCH ACROSS THE NEEDLE ONE TIME IS A ROW.

SO THERE WILL BE NO ERROR IN READING PATTERNS, PLEASE NOTICE THAT IF WE MEAN "ROWS", WE WILL SAY, "ROWS", LIKE "K 2 ROWS". IF INSTRUCTIONS ARE WRITTEN K 2 OR P 2, THIS WILL MEAN INDIVIDUAL STITCHES, AS K 2 STITCHES OR P 2 STITCHES.

BEFORE BEGINNING A ROW, PULL SUFFICIENT YARN FROM BALL TO MAKE A ROW. THIS WILL ALLOW YARN TO SLIDE EASILY THROUGH FINGERS AND ELIMINATE TOO MUCH PULL ON THE YARN.

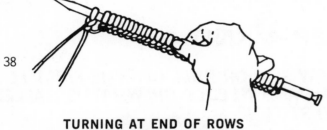

38

TURNING AT END OF ROWS

WHEN YOU HAVE FINISHED WORKING A ROW OF THE KNIT STITCH, YARN WILL FINISH HANGING AT THE BACK OF THE PIECE.

KNIT TIP: ALWAYS LEAVE YARN ON THE SAME SIDE OF PIECE ON WHICH IT FINISHES.

TO WORK SECOND AND SUCCEEDING ROWS, TAKE THE RIGHT HAND NEEDLE CONTAINING THE YARN, TURN AND PLACE IN LEFT HAND. 39 PLEASE NOTE THE YARN IS NOW HANGING ON THE FRONT SIDE. DO NOT DISTURB THIS.

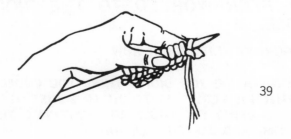

39

IT IS EASIER TO BEGIN EACH ROW BY INSERTING NEEDLE IN FIRST STITCH, LEFT HAND HOLDING BOTH NEEDLES 33 , AND THEN PICKING UP YARN ON PROPER FINGERS OF RIGHT HAND. 28

AS YOU KNIT THIS FIRST STITCH, NOTE THAT YARN RETURNS TO <u>BACK</u> OF WORK. CONTINUE TO KNIT EACH STITCH ACROSS ROW.

GARTER STITCH 40

GARTER STITCH PATTERN: KNIT EACH STITCH ACROSS EVERY ROW.

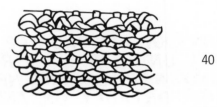

40

PRACTICE: WORK THE KNIT STITCH FOR 6 ROWS.

HOW TO RECOGNIZE A KNIT STITCH

THE KNIT STITCH IS A FLAT, SMOOTH V-SHAPED STITCH.

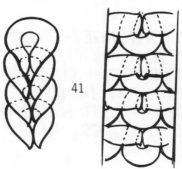

41

Looking at one side of this knitting, you will notice in the Garter stitch pattern, every other row is a ridge. When making a knit stitch, the opposite side of the stitch (a purl stitch) is a U-shaped, horizontal, nubby, rough stitch. 41

The knit stitch, as you make it, is smooth on the side facing you and rough on the back. However, when you turn to work the next row, the rough (purl stitch) will show and many knitters believe this is the knit stitch. This is incorrect.

IN GARTER STITCH, A RIDGE IS MADE BY KNITTING TWO ROWS.

AFTER WORKING SEVERAL ROWS, YOU WILL NOTE KNITTED PIECE HAS THE SAME PATTERN ON BOTH SIDES. AN EXACT COUNT OF THE ROWS KNITTED CAN BE MADE BY COUNTING EACH RIDGE ON BOTH SIDES OF THE PIECE.

PRACTICE: CONTINUE IN GARTER STITCH PATTERN ON THESE 24 STITCHES UNTIL PIECE MEASURES ABOUT 6" FROM BEGINNING OR AT LEAST 3" HAVE BEEN KNITTED WITHOUT MISTAKES.

A "MUST" REMINDER FOR SUCCESSFUL KNITTING: SEE 35 *AND BE SURE THE SECOND FINGER AND THUMB OF RIGHT HAND REMAIN ON THE NEEDLE AT ALL TIMES, EXCEPT WHEN THE RIGHT HAND IS NEEDED TO WRAP NEEDLE FOR NEXT STITCH.*

SOME KNIT TIPS FOR KNITTING PROBLEMS

GAINING EXTRA STITCHES AT BEGINNING OF KNIT ROWS

When this occurs, you are probably doing one of the following:

1. After turning needles to work another row, you are putting the yarn end OVER TOP of the needle and to back. 42 When you

do this, note that you have TWO loops on top of needle, where you had only ONE before.

WRONG-EXTRA STITCH   **RIGHT**

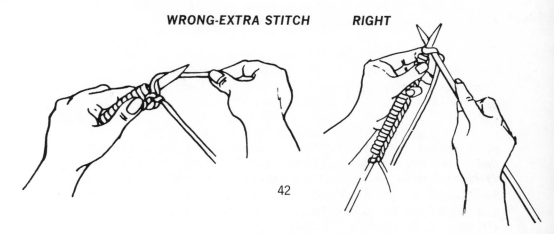

42

To correct this: Leave yarn on side of needle where it finishes and as you knit the first stitch on needle, yarn will go around, under tip of needle and to back of work as you make a knit stitch.

KNIT TIP: ANYTIME YOU PLACE YARN OVER TOP OF A NEEDLE, YOU WILL HAVE A NEW OR EXTRA STITCH ON NEXT ROW.

2. Or, as you begin to knit the second row, many times the first stitch will have a long loose loop under it. DO NOT KNIT THIS LOOP for you will gain an extra stitch. 43

KNIT ONLY LOOPS ON NEEDLE.
DO   **DON'T**

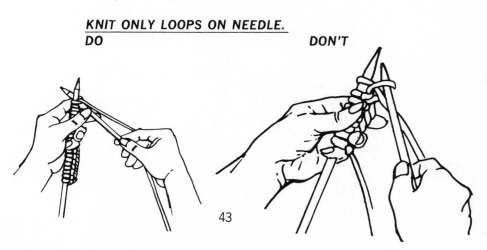

43

FEEDING NEW STITCHES WITH LEFT HAND

AS THE "OLD STITCH" IS PULLED OFF, IT IS NECESSARY THAT THE LEFT HAND PUSH UP A NEW STITCH.

We need to coordinate our hand movements to do this. This is like two men working together on an assembly line. As one finishes with one item, the other man immediately feeds the next item so there will be no waste of space, time or motion.

THE BEST WAY TO PRACTICE THIS IS: AFTER YOU SCOOP UP NEW STITCH , WITH THE LEFT HAND PULL BACK THUMB AND FIRST FINGER AND WITH ONE MOTION, PULL OFF THE OLD STITCH WITH THE RIGHT NEEDLE AND PUSH UP THE NEW STITCH BY JUST STRAIGHTENING OUT THE FINGERS OF LEFT HAND. THIS IS A VERY EASY MOTION WITH LITTLE EFFORT AND WILL BECOME AUTOMATIC AFTER A LITTLE PRACTICE.

ADJUSTING STITCHES ON NEEDLES

FREQUENTLY IT WILL BE NECESSARY TO MOVE A NEW GROUP OF STITCHES UP TO THE END OF LEFT NEEDLE. TO KEEP FROM LOSING STITCHES, HAVE RIGHT HAND REACH UP, HOLD BOTH NEEDLES, AND HOLD TIP OF LEFT NEEDLE WITH THUMB AND INDEX FINGER. PUSH UP STITCHES. 44

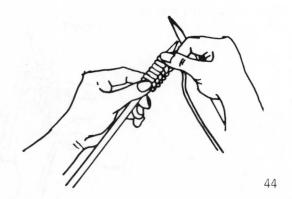

44

WHEN STITCHES NEED TO BE ADJUSTED ON THE LEFT NEEDLE, USUALLY RIGHT HAND NEEDLE IS "CRAMMED" WITH STITCHES. TAKE BOTH NEEDLES IN LEFT HAND. WITH THUMB AND INDEX FINGERS ON LEFT HAND HOLDING TIP OF RIGHT NEEDLE, SMOOTH THE STITCHES DOWN THE RIGHT NEEDLE AND OUT OF WAY. 45

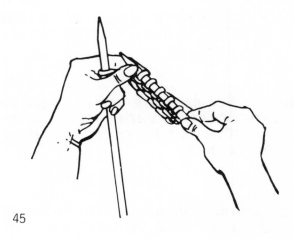

45

Some knitters adjust the stitches on either needle by pushing down on the tips of the needles. This is not a good idea for beginners since it makes the fingers sore, requires more hand motion and makes it easy to lose stitches off end of needle.

RHYTHM IN KNITTING

GOOD KNITTING WILL HAVE A REGULAR RHYTHM IN WORKING THE STITCHES.

Beginners should count slowly and evenly 1-2-3-4, like a steady dance rhythm, as you do the four steps for the knit stitch. After the stitch becomes easy to make, Steps 3 and 4 will be worked as one count and the stitch is made in a rhythm of 1-2-3, like waltz time. Rhythm and regularity of motions will make easy and even knitting.

LOSING NEEDLE OUT OF WORK AT BEGINNING OF ROWS

Beginners often lose the needle out of their knitting on the first or second stitches of a row. To help this, I often rest the right hand needle on top of the right forearm until several stitches have been worked onto needle. Then drop needle to lap and continue as usual.

RIGHT NEEDLE IN RIGHT HAND WHEN RESUMING KNITTING

If you stop knitting in the middle of a row, when starting again, put needle with the ball of yarn attached in right hand. Stitches on this needle have already been worked. Continue across row.

If this is done incorrectly, you will have more rows of knitting on one side of the piece than on the other, as well as a hole where this section began. 46

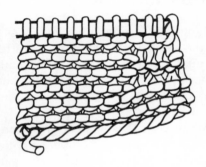

46

SHORT ROWS

WHEN WORK IS "DELIBERATELY" TURNED WITHIN THE ROW, IT IS CALLED "KNITTING WITH SHORT ROWS". 47

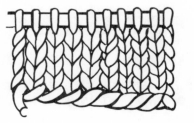

47

THIS IS DONE WHERE MORE DEPTH OR FULLNESS IS REQUIRED IN A SECTION OF A ROW. PATTERNS WILL INSTRUCT YOU TO TURN AT SPECIFIC PLACES, MAKING THAT SECTION OF THE PIECE LONGER THAN THE REST OF THE ROW. This principle is used in making heels of socks, collars, baby sweater yokes, shawls, stoles, seats of pants, bathing suits, etc.

TENSION

TENSION IS THE TIGHTNESS WITH WHICH YARN IS HELD WHILE MAKING STITCHES.

REMEMBER THAT YOU ARE MAKING FABRIC.

Yarn tension can be compared to the tension on a sewing machine. If the tension is too loose, you get loose stitches which make "sleazy" limp material that will not hold its shape. This is most unsatisfactory in knitting.

If tension is too tight, you get rigid seams in sewing and in knitting all the "bounce" or life in the yarn will be stretched out of it and it will become hard or "like a board".

If the yarn is held properly, you will feel a good pull or "tugging" to the yarn and when yarn is released, it will "mesh" and be of tight enough weave to hold its shape for size and wear.

PLEASE KEEP TENSION ON ALL KINDS OF YARNS.

Many knitters will be fascinated with the beautiful yarns, especially those that are soft and lovely, like mohairs, and will just "lay" the yarn around the needles. MOHAIR SWEATERS WILL NOT STRETCH IF KNITTED WITH PROPER TENSION. Of course, if yarn is fed in limply, ANY material used will drop and stretch.

THE INDIVIDUAL'S TENSION

Each of you has her own individual tension, just as you have your individual handwriting. I never change anyone's manner of knitting if they have good tension and no knitting problems. But your own basic tension must be established before you can begin to work out stitch gauge which determines the SIZE of pieces of knitting.

There are many knitters whose tension is average and they have no problems of sizing knitted pieces. Others have natural tensions that may be loose and some that may be tight.

DO NOT CHANGE YOUR NATURAL TENSION WHEN IT IS CORRECT. CHANGE THE SIZE OF NEEDLES TO GET STITCH GAUGE.

My knitting tension is on the "loose" side. In other words, garments would come out larger than size indicated. I get perfect gauge by using one size smaller needles than patterns call for. One of my knitters knits very tightly and usually uses two sizes larger needles than pattern calls for.

People tell me they can knit tight, loose, or any tension. I DO NOT BELIEVE THAT ANYONE CAN CONSISTENTLY KNIT TIGHTER OR LOOSER THAN THEIR NATURAL TENSION FOR AN ENTIRE SWEATER AND DO A FINE JOB. Certainly, it would be no fun to have to think of how tight or loose to pull every stitch of a sweater.

Illustration 48 shows the difference of individual knitting of three knitters using the same number of stitches, same yarn and same size needles.

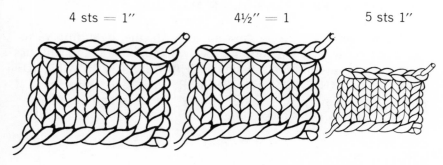

| 4 sts = 1″ | 4½″ = 1 | 5 sts 1″ |

48

Therefore, if gauge to make correct size was 4½ sts to 1″, the knitter who knitted 5 sts to 1″, would need a LARGER needle and the knitter who knitted 4 sts to 1″, would need a smaller needle to get 4½ sts to 1″. This does not concern you too much at this time as a beginner for items to be made do not require an exact fit. This information, however, is very important when making sweaters, suits, coats, etc., which you will do later.

EFFECTS OF YOUR PHYSICAL AND NERVOUS SYSTEM ON YOUR KNITTING

Knitting is a very personal thing and in numerous instances I have seen the state of health or the nervous condition of a knitter decide the degree of tension and quality of the knitting — it usually becoming loose, large and very uneven, making garment too big and ill-fitting.

Or to the other extreme. where nervous tensions and irritations are taken out on the yarn and it is yanked and pulled very tightly, wool becomes stiff and heavy, "like a board" and usually the garment will be too small.

If you have a similar problem and correct sizing of pieces needs to be done, put knitting aside until you are feeling better, then your knitting will more likely be smooth and even. This works quite well.

GAUGE

GAUGE IS MEASUREMENT.

GAUGE IS THE NUMBER OF STITCHES PER INCH IN WIDTH AND THE NUMBER OF ROWS PER INCH IN HEIGHT. 49

49

STITCHES PER INCH

In knitting we are given a specific number of stitches to be knitted in a specific number of inches. Therefore, we must knit the stitches the correct size to make our piece of knitting the correct width in inches. Your knitting pattern will tell you the recommended needle size.

EXAMPLE:
MAN'S SWEATER, SIZE 40
1 pair No. 8 needles
GAUGE: 5 sts = 1"
                6 rows = 1"

This sweater pattern calls for 100 stitches to be used for the back. To be knitted the correct width, you must knit 5 sts in each inch. Since we have 100 stitches and the gauge is 5 sts to 1", divide 100 by 5 and we get a width of 20".

TO COMPUTE CORRECT WIDTH IN INCHES:

NUMBER OF STITCHES
(ACROSS KNITTED PIECE)

DIVIDED BY

STITCH GAUGE (STITCHES PER ONE INCH)

EQUALS

INCHES (IN WIDTH)

However, if your piece measures 21" or more, stitches are too large and you should use needles at least one size smaller than recommended. If your piece measures 19" or under, stitches are too small and you should use needles at least one size larger than recommended.

IF YOU ARE UNABLE TO GET STITCH GAUGE BY USING NEEDLES ONE OR TWO SIZES LARGER OR SMALLER, YOUR TENSION NEEDS CORRECTING.

ROWS PER INCH

If measurements of length (up and down) is done by inches, use a tape measure or ruler, measuring UP TO THE NEEDLE, and do not worry too much about gauge for rows.

However, the number of rows per inch do become important in raglan sleeves when they determine the length of the sleeve cap and in patterns that are worked entirely by rows. You can understand that a loose knitter would have FEWER rows in one inch (bigger stitches), the extra rows would make more length than desired and knitted piece would be longer. There is no great harm in this unless gauge is way off or if piece would be just too long for a short or small person.

If the person knitted on the "tight" side, piece would be shorter since rows would be closer together and the inches in length used up faster.

In these instances, work for gauge in rows and then pick size of garment that will fit you in width.

ADJUSTMENT TO GET GAUGE

FIRST CHECK AND CORRECT ANY TENSION PROBLEMS. WITHOUT PROPER TENSION IT IS IMPOSSIBLE TO GET PROPER GAUGE.

SECOND, CHANGE TO NEEDLES OF A LARGER OR SMALLER SIZE UNTIL CORRECT GAUGE IS SECURED.

When you begin knitting sweaters, you will make a 3" or 4" yarn sample of the pattern stitch, usually called a "swatch" or "test piece", and measure it to determine if the needles are the correct size for you to make proper gauge. This, in turn, assures you the finished knitted garment will be the size you selected to make for your pattern.

SOME HABITS THAT CAUSE TOO TIGHT KNITTING

1. DON'T KNIT ON THE TIPS OF THE NEEDLES.

DO be sure when you make your stitch that the right hand needle is pushed up and through the new stitch until it gets to the largest or "fat" part of the needle. 36 This is called "sizing" the stitch. If you insist on knitting on the tips of the needles, there is no object in using different sizes of needles to make different size stitches.

2. DON'T ALLOW INDEX FINGER TO SHOOT UP IN THE AIR TO TAKE UP SLACK YARN. 50

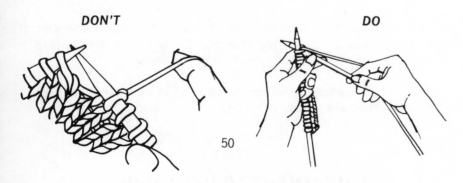

DON'T   **DO**

50

It is instinctive to "take up the slack" in yarn by shooting the finger in the air, when yarn is limp or the hand has been placed too close to point of needle.

If you do this, hand will become tired easily and the loop on the needle will be quite tight. Notice it covers only about half of the needle, instead of circling the needle and making a full loop. Whenever you have tighter or small loops, you will have smaller garments.

DO always after wrapping yarn around needle, swing to end of yarn and immediately place index finger and thumb on right hand needle. 35 This will make each stitch exactly alike in size and tension.

3. DON'T ALLOW THUMB TO HOLD YARN WHEN WRAPPING.

The thumb should NEVER touch the yarn you wrap or knit with. The thumb is very heavy, strong and has tendency to pull the yarn very tight and cut stitch in half. 51

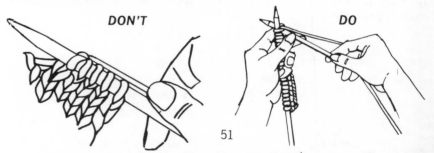

DON'T   **DO**

51

4. DON'T PULL OR SQUEEZE THE YARN TOO HARD WITH RIGHT HAND WHEN WRAPPING.

DO allow yarn to slip through fingers more easily.

5. DON'T WORRY IF YOUR NATURAL TENSION MAKES SMALLER STITCHES THAN REQUIRED TO MAKE KNITS THE CORRECT SIZE.

DO use one size larger needles. Extreme cases have found it necessary to use two, or even three, sizes larger needles to get correct size pieces of knitting.

6. DON'T HAVE ANY TIGHT PULLING OF YARN FROM BALL.

DO pull out sufficient yarn for a row, thus allowing yarn to slide freely on right hand.

SOME HABITS THAT CAUSE TOO LOOSE KNITTING

1. DON'T ALLOW YARN TO SLIDE THROUGH FINGERS TOO EASILY.

DO cup fingers and hold third, fourth and fifth fingers closer together. 28

A SECOND WAY TO HOLD YARN WITH RIGHT HAND

Some knitters, because of thin fingers, large spaces between their fingers or the special structure of their hands, can't control or hold the yarn tight enough. With this situation, try holding yarn with the second and fifth fingers as follows:

To pick up yarn, place the little finger on top of yarn, go under and over yarn, thus making a loop around little finger. Then pick up yarn on top of second finger between first kunckle and finger-nail. 52

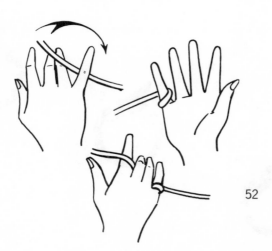

52

I recommend this method of holding yarn ONLY if the first method 28 is unsatisfactory. Yarn does not slide too easily with this method of holding but on some materials that are "slippery", such as cotton, linen, silk and some synthetics, this method of holding is excellent and necessary.

2. DON'T ALLOW YARN TO BE LOOSE AND LIMP.

The knitting will be too big in size, limp, lack "bounce", not hold its shape for proper sizing and will be difficult to make garment retain size after washing. All this is caused by too loose tension.

DO after wrapping thread around needle for stitch, be sure to swing to end of yarn HAVING A PULLING OR TUGGING FEELING BEFORE PLACING RIGHT HAND ON NEEDLE. 34 You will not hurt the yarn. This will keep yarn tense so knitting will "mesh" together and have a good "bounce".

3. DON'T WORRY IF YOUR NATURAL TENSION MAKES LARGER STITCHES THAN REQUIRED TO MAKE KNITS THE CORRECT SIZE.

Do use one size smaller needles. Extreme cases have found it necessary to use two, or even three, sizes smaller needles to get correct sized pieces of knitting.

LEFT-HANDED KNITTERS

In teaching beginners, whether right-handed or left-handed, use this right-handed "English" method as presented. Most left-handed persons today are ambidextrous. In fact, some of the loveliest knitting has been done by left-handed people, knitting in right-handed fashion. This was accomplished through careful attention to details.

Only very extreme cases should knit left-handed, which requires reversing "positions" of all stitches and yarn. If the knitter, within five to ten minutes of trying right-handed knitting, becomes nauseated or very frustrated, then by all means knit left-handed. Knitting should be enjoyed!

To knit left-handed:

1. When being instructed by a right-handed person, have instructress sit FACING YOU. Do the same motions as she does, using hands that are exactly across from hers, that it, your right hand like her left hand and your left hand like her right.

2. In using pictures, place them facing a mirror. This will reverse pictures and you will knit as pictured in mirror.

3. If following word instructions, substitute the word right for left and left for right.

MISTAKES AND EXTRA STITCHES

You no doubt will make some mistakes and acquire extra stitches. Do not be alarmed, for you are learning and, of course, will not knit perfectly at this time.

If you do wish to practice the knit stitch more before learning the purl stitch, continue to work on this same piece. The number of stitches on the needle is unimportant at this time. Also, after learning this stitch without mistakes, some beginners like to start again, cast on 24 stitches and work 6 rows of Garter stitch before going on to the next stitch.

Others like to keep their first knitting and over the years each time a new stitch is learned, work 2" or 3" of pattern stitch onto the strip. This is a common practice in Europe and makes an interesting record of your progress in the art of handknitting.

HOW TO CORRECT MISTAKES

By this time you have knitted a nice length, which could be continued to make a neck scarf, an ear-warmer, baby doll cover, shoe shine cloth, hot dish pad, etc. But, — you have made some mistakes and would like to be able to correct them. In fact, you may already have rearranged the loops correctly by experimenting. Most beginners become alarmed with their first mistakes but are more afraid of losing stitches off the needle rather than trying to correct mistakes.

IF YOU "DROP A STITCH", THAT IS, HAVE A LOOSE LOOP OFF A NEEDLE, IMMEDIATELY PLACE LOOP BACK ON NEEDLE OR STITCH HOLDER OR RUN A THREAD THROUGH IT SO IT WILL NOT RAVEL OR RUN DOWN MORE.

HOW TO CORRECT STITCHES BY TAKING OUT ROWS

Until you have ability to go down through rows below the needles, pick up and correct single stitches, the easiest way for beginners to correct mistakes is to take out stitches one by one, row by row, until all mistakes are corrected.

WE ARE GOING TO UNDO STITCHES ONE AT A TIME.

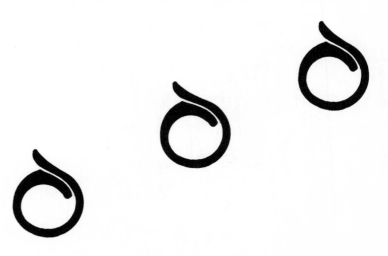

TURN WORK AROUND SO NEEDLES ARE SWITCHED TO THE OPPOSITE HANDS, THUS PUTTING NEEDLE WITH YARN ATTACHED IN LEFT HAND AND SECOND NEEDLE IN RIGHT HAND.

THREAD YARN OVER SECOND AND FOURTH FINGERS ON RIGHT HAND AS USUAL. BRING YARN BETWEEN THE TWO NEEDLES TO THE FRONT OF WORK AND LIFT THE RIGHT HAND INDEX FINGER INTO THE AIR SO THAT THREAD FROM LEFT NEEDLE IS PULLED TIGHTLY. 53 THIS IS DONE SO THAT YOU MAY RAISE THE YARN AND PULL IT TIGHT, TO SEE WHERE THE YARN COMES OUT OF THE PREVIOUS STITCH.

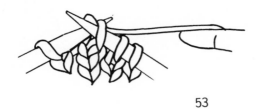

53

NOTE: THIS IS THE ONLY TIME IN MY METHOD OF TEACHING THAT THE RIGHT INDEX FINGER IS ALLOWED TO REMAIN OFF THE RIGHT HAND NEEDLE AND "SHOOTS" IN THE AIR.

*TAKE RIGHT NEEDLE AND FROM THE BACK OF THE WORK, PUT NEEDLE IN CENTER OF STITCH WHERE THE YARN COMES OUT. THIS WILL BE IN THE FIRST ROW UNDER STITCH ON NEEDLE. (53)

SLIP THIS STITCH OFF LEFT NEEDLE TO RIGHT NEEDLE, PULLING YARN OUT OF THE STITCH. ONE STITCH HAS BEEN UNDONE. (ALWAYS RETURN YARN TO FRONT OF WORK BEFORE UNDOING NEXT STITCH).

REPEAT FROM * UNTIL ALL MISTAKES ARE CORRECTED.

WHEN YOU COME TO A LOOP ON THE LEFT NEEDLE THAT DOES NOT HAVE THE END OF THE YARN IN IT, THIS IS THE DROPPED OR UNWORKED STITCH. SLIP THIS TO THE RIGHT NEEDLE WITH THE RIGHT SIDE OF THE LOOP ON TOP. TURN WORK (WHICH WILL SWITCH NEEDLES TO CORRECT HANDS) AND RESUME KNITTING AS PER INSTRUCTIONS.

Or, if you wish to correct mistakes from the same side on which you were knitting, left needles would be inserted in FRONT of stitch below one on right needle. Slip off, pull out yarn and proceed as per instructions. This method of undoing stitches is often easier for left-handed persons.

TO PICK UP STITCHES WHEN NEEDLE HAS BEEN REMOVED FROM ROW OF STITCHES

If error is several rows down in knitting, pull work off needle. Unravel to within ONE ROW of error.

Holding knitted piece in left hand, *pull yarn from first stitch. Insert right needle from BACK into center of stitch. Repeat between *'s across row until all stitches have been replaced on needle. Turn and resume pattern. 54

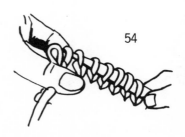

54

HOW TO CORRECT EXTRA STITCHES IN ROWS OF KNITTING

1. A common error made by beginning knitters is to wrap yarn around needle and pull off old stitch without scooping up loop for new stitch. 55 Therefore, you will have an extra loop on needle and if this is not corrected, next row will not only have an extra stitch, but there will be a hole in the knitting. 56 Undo as many stitches and as many rows as necessary to correct this.

 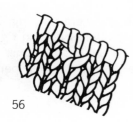

55   56

2. When inserting needle to knit, be sure you use only the LOOP ON NEEDLE. It is easy to get too far down in knitting and pick up loop from the rows below. This will pucker the knitting and, depending on how you work this stitch, many times extra loops are found in the next row. Always correct mistakes.

3. Split yarns should always be fixed immediately. 58 They cannot be corrected later. Also you will have a weak spot in your knitting where yarn is split. To eliminate split yarns, always insert needle UNDER other needle. 57

DO NOT INSERT NEEDLE AGAINST YARN.

_DO_   **_DON'T_**

57   58

Turn work to the side that shows the stitches as knits. Insert a crochet hook in the dropped stitch loop and *placing hook under next thread above, pull the horizontal thread through the loop to the front. Repeat from * until corrected and all rows of thread have been picked up. Replace loop on proper needle.

 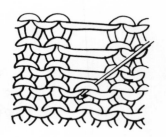

59

60

TO CORRECT PURLWISE SINGLE STITCH DROPPED DOWN SEVERAL ROWS IN STOCKINETTE STITCH 60

Although more awkward, purl stitches can be picked up from the purl side, but it is easier to turn work and correct this on the knit side.

TO PICK UP STITCH DROPPED DOWN SEVERAL ROWS IN PATTERN STITCH

A good knowledge of the pattern stitch is needed to pick up stitches down through several rows of knitting. With practice, this can be done satisfactorily.

Sometimes, however, the picked up stitches work in loosely or tightly and do not match the tension of the rest of the knitting. 61 It is then advisable to undo the knitting to where error occurred and re-knit.

61

62

If the stitch has been dropped very far down in knitting and knitter does not wish to re-knit the piece, fasten the loop at that point, rather than to pick up the stitch through a lot of rows. 62 Catching and fastening the loop is the lesser of the two evils here.

DROPPED STITCHES

TO CORRECT KNITWISE A SINGLE STITCH DROPPED ONE ROW 63

63

Place the loop of the dropped stitch on the left needle with the long loose piece of yarn to the RIGHT of the mistake.

Take right needle and from the front of work, lift the dropped stitch OVER the longer piece of yarn and OFF the end of the needle.

Stitch is now corrected. Put on proper needle and proceed.

TO CORRECT PURLWISE A SINGLE STITCH DROPPED ONE ROW 64

64

Place loop from dropped stitch to left of first stitch on left needle.

Insert right needle from back through center of first stitch and on top of the loose loop.

Push loop out and down as if to purl.

Turn loop so right side of loop is on top.

PURL STITCH

NOW WE WILL LEARN TO MAKE THE "PURL" STITCH. 65

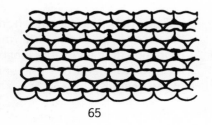

65

THIS IS A NUBBY, ROUGH STITCH THAT LAYS HORIZONTALLY ALONG NEEDLE AND WILL BE WORKED TO SHOW ON THE SIDE OF THE PIECE FACING YOU. (YOU WILL NOTE THE BACK OF A PURL STITCH IS A KNIT STITCH.)

PLACE KNITTED PIECE IN LEFT HAND. YARN MUST BE ON FRONT OF WORK. NEEDLES AND YARN ARE HELD IN THE SAME MANNER AS FOR THE KNIT STITCH.

STEP 1 PURL 66

66

SLIP THE RIGHT HAND NEEDLE STRAIGHT IN THE RIGHT SIDE OF THE FIRST LOOP ON LEFT NEEDLE AND CROSS TO THE FRONT OF THE NEEDLE, MAKING AN "X" WITH THE NEEDLE POINTS.

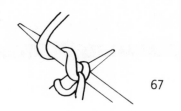

67

STEP 2 PURL 67 68

TAKE BOTH NEEDLES IN LEFT HAND.

WRAP YARN STRAIGHT DOWN TOWARD FLOOR (BETWEEN THE TWO NEEDLES) AND TO THE LEFT AROUND NEEDLE (COUNTER-CLOCK-WISE).

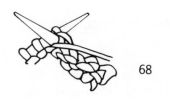

68

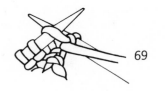

69

STEP 3 PURL 69

WITH RIGHT NEEDLE, PUSH YARN DOWN AND AWAY FROM YOU SO NEW STITCH COMES OUT AT BACK OF WORK.

70

STEP 4 PURL 70

PULL OFF OLD STITCH. ONE PURL STITCH HAS BEEN MADE.

PURL EACH STITCH ACROSS ROW BY REPEATING STEPS 1-2-3-4 PURL. 71

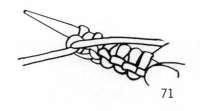

71

PRACTICE: WORK EVERY ROW IN PURL STITCH UNTIL PIECE MEASURES ABOUT 3". YOU ARE GETTING THE SAME KIND OF PATTERN OF RIDGES AS WHEN YOU KNITTED EVERY ROW IN GARTER STITCH. 40

This is because you are putting the purl stitch first on one side and then on the other. Although at times it might be necessary to make ridges purlwise, Garter stitch is easier and usually done knitwise.

CHECK THESE PURL STITCHES. ARE THE STITCHES EVEN? ARE THERE ANY MISTAKES? HAVE YOU GAINED EXTRA STITCHES?

IF PURL STITCHES ARE LOOSER THAN KNIT STITCHES

Do not be alarmed if this section of purl stitches is looser and wider than the same number of stitches in a knit section. This often happens on purl stitches, evidently because the yarn is allowed to slip through the hand more loosely. This seems to be caused by the position of the hand and arm having less control of the yarn in making purl stitch motions. With practice and experience, your purl stitch will be uniform with the knit stitch.

KNIT TIP: BE AWARE THAT YOU MAY NEED TO HOLD THE YARN A LITTLE TIGHTER OR FIRMER WHEN MAKING THE PURL STITCH, BUT PLEASE DON'T GO TO EXTREMES. CORRECT ALL MISTAKES.

GAINING EXTRA STITCHES AT BEGINNING OF PURL ROWS

But you say, "I have gained extra stitches!" or "I made two loops on the first stitch!" This is a common error with beginners.

AT THE BEGINNING OF THE PURL ROW, BEFORE WRAPPING YARN AROUND NEEDLE, YOU MUST HAVE THE YARN COMING STRAIGHT OUT OF END OF PREVIOUS ROW. YARN CANNOT BE WRAPPED AROUND OR OVER TOP OF RIGHT NEEDLE. MOST KNITTERS ERR IN PICKING UP THE YARN AND BRINGING IT OVER TOP OF THE NEEDLE FROM BACK TO FRONT BEFORE WRAPPING. 72

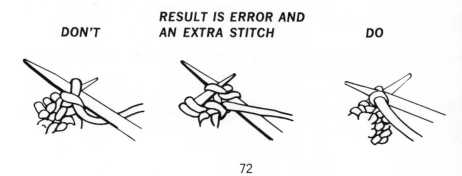

DON'T   **RESULT IS ERROR AND AN EXTRA STITCH**   **DO**

72

KNIT TIP: ANYTIME YOU LAY YARN ACROSS TOP OF THE NEEDLE, YOU WILL GAIN A NEW OR EXTRA STITCH ON THE NEXT ROW. 73

DON'T

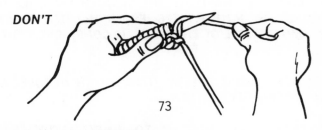

73

To pick up yarn correctly:

1. Put needle in right front of the first stitch, reach under right needle for yarn and bring to front side of work. Pick up yarn to work stitch. YARN MUST COME STRAIGHT OUT OF END STITCH. 66

2. Or, a quicker way is to take right hand needle and from the FRONT, put tip of needle under the yarn, thus placing yarn on top of needle, and insert needle in right front of stitch.   Right hand then can easily pick up yarn from top of needle eliminating errors and extra stitches.

STOCKINETTE STITCH

SO FAR WE HAVE BEEN DOING THE SAME STITCH ACROSS EACH ROW. NOW WE ARE GOING TO USE DIFFERENT STITCHES ON DIFFERENT ROWS.

WHEN YOU KNIT A ROW, A RIDGE IS MADE ON THE BACK OF THE PIECE. WHEN YOU PURL A ROW, A RIDGE IS MADE ON THE FRONT OF THE PIECE.

STOCKINETTE STITCH IS MADE BY ALTERNATING ONE KNIT ROW AND ONE PURL ROW. 74

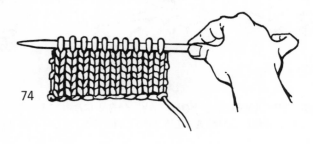

74

YOU WILL THEN HAVE ALL THE SMOOTH STITCHES ON ONE SIDE AND ALL THE ROUGH STITCHES ON THE OTHER SIDE. THE KNIT, OR SMOOTH SIDE OF THE PIECE, IS CONSIDERED THE RIGHT SIDE.

PRACTICE: USING THE 24 STITCHES ON NEEDLE, WORK 6 ROWS IN STOCKINETTE STITCH.

TWO EXAMPLES OF WRITING STOCKINETTE STITCH PATTERN:

No. 1

Row 1: K across row.
Row 2: P across row.
Repeat these 2 rows for pattern.

No. 2

*K 1 row, P 1 row.
Repeat between *'s for pattern.

Stockinette stitch is also called "flat knitting" and most of our pattern stitches, motifs and laces are built on this basic stitch.

REVERSE STOCKINETTE STITCH

REVERSE STOCKINETTE IS THE PURL SIDE OF STOCKINETTE USED AS THE RIGHT SIDE OF THE KNITTED ITEM. 75

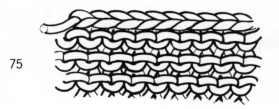

75

Pattern Stitch would be written as follows:

REVERSE STOCKINETTE STITCH

Row 1: P across row.
Row 2: K across row.
Repeat these two rows for pattern.

Quaker Rib pattern is an example of alternating 3 rows of Stockinette and 3 rows of Reverse Stockinette.

UNEVENNESS OF ROWS IN STOCKINETTE STITCH
76

It is difficult for some knitters to work Stockinette stitch evenly. To check your work, inspect the purl side and if you have definite lines every other row, usually the PURL ROWS are being worked looser than the knit rows. For left-handed knitters it will probably be the knit row that is too loose.

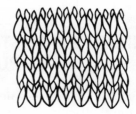

76

On the right side of this piece, the knit stitches will be uneven every other row but the unevenness will not be as noticeable as on the purl side. This irregularity is particulary obvious and undesirable on large bulkies.

TO CORRECT:

1. On the purl row tighten the tension of your yarn a little by holding yarn tighter and not allowing yarn to slide through the fingers quite so easily.

2. When wrapping yarn around needle for stitch, swing down until yarn is pulled a little tighter BEFORE replacing right hand on needle. You should feel a little more "tugging" on the yarn. 34

3. Some knitters never overcome this difference in stitch size. Extreme cases can be quite successful in correcting this problem by using one needle of the required size for the knit row and one needle of a smaller size for the purl row, as: One No. 10 needle in the right hand for the knit row and one No. 9 needle in the left hand for the purl row.

UNEVENNESS OF STITCHES IN STOCKINETTE STITCH

If the purl side shows streaks of loose knitting that are scattered over the piece irregularly, this means that you are not feeding the stitches on the left hand needle regularly. You are not pushing up new stitches often enough so the same distance and tension will occur between each new stitch made.

EDGES OF ROWS

Most beginners fuss about the edges of their knitting. If the first two stitches are of the same size and evenness as the rest of the row, you have no worry.

Often one edge, as on Stockinette stitch, will be very nice and the other loose and spreading. Careful control of tension will help but not necessarily overcome the "human factor" which seems to be the only answer as to why this sometimes happens. Many times this problem cannot be solved to the knitter's satisfaction. The difference in edges of Stockinette stitch is not too important since they are usually sewed into seams, crocheted on the edges or trimmed. This takes care of any difference in length of edges.

BASIC DON'TS FOR EDGES OF ROWS

Some knitters do various and unusual things to the edges of rows. Perhaps, these ideas might be useful for special effects but I have no use for these ideas for BASIC KNITTING.

1. DON'T SLIP STITCHES at beginning or end of rows, unless necessary to make pattern. It is almost impossible to sew a good seam with slip stitch edges.

2. DON'T WEAVE YARN between or around, before or after end stitches to make tight edges. This makes very rigid and undesirable seams.

3. DON'T INTERRUPT PATTERN by knitting the first and last stitch of every row. This makes rough edges which are difficult to sew and result in thick, bulky seams.

JOINING YARNS

You will join yarns when:

1. You need to start a new ball.

2. You need to cut a knot out of the yarn.

3. You do not have enough yarn to work a complete row.

HOW MUCH YARN TO WORK ONE ROW?

It is a good habit to pull out enough yarn to make a row. Inspect it. If there is a knot in the yarn or if you are not sure if you have enough yarn to finish the row, measure as follows:

LAY YARN LOOSELY ACROSS KNITTED PIECE THREE TIMES.
77 *THIS WILL MAKE ONE ROW OF STOCKINETTE STITCH.*

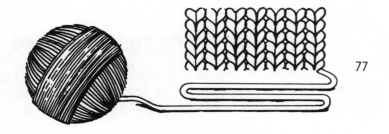

77

WHERE THERE ARE CABLES OR PATTERNS THAT WOULD USE MORE YARN, LAY LOOSELY ACROSS ROW FOUR TIMES.

WHERE TO JOIN YARNS?

DO NOT JOIN YARNS OR LEAVE ANY KNOTS IN THE MIDDLE OF ROWS. 78

DON'T

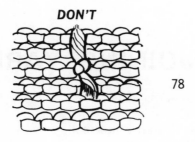

78

FOR BASIC KNITTING OF FLAT PIECES, I RECOMMEND THAT JOINING YARNS BE DONE ON THE EDGES.

Exception: In our beginning items to be knitted, like the scarves and blankets, with Garter or Seed stitch borders, do NOT join on edges, because joinings would be bumpy and difficult to hide. Join at the inside border edge or where any rough texture will allow weaving of ends without showing.

Joining on circular knitting, as for a skirt, presents a difficult problem and manner of joining will depend on the kind, texture and size of yarn used. You will need to experiment with the four methods of joining described and use your own judgement as to which would give the smoothest and best results.

HOW TO JOIN YARNS ?

1. SLIP LOOP (I prefer this method.)

LEAVING A 5″ END, CUT YARN. 79

CUT KNOT FROM YARN OR PICK UP A NEW BALL. (SAVE ALL PIECES OF YARN FOR YOU WILL USE THESE IN SEWING SEAMS AND THERE WILL BE NO WASTE OF YARN.) PLACE END OF NEW BALL AROUND END OF OLD YARN AND MAKE ONE LOOP ONLY.
80

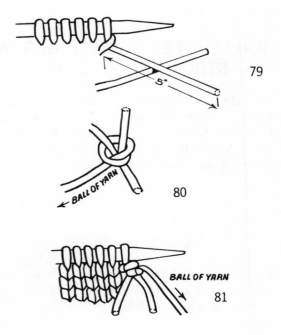

SLIDE THIS KNOT UP TO THE EDGE OF KNITTING 81 AND CONTINUE KNITTING. AFTER KNITTING HAS BEEN FINISHED, ENDS WILL BE PULLED UP TO FIT EDGE OF PIECE, TIED INTO A SQUARE KNOT AND AFTER SEAMS HAVE BEEN SEWED, ENDS WOVEN INTO SEAMS.

2. OVERLAP ENDS.

Overlap the end of old yarn and end of new yarn about 4". Knitting with the double thickness, work 3 or 4 sts. 82 On the next row, work each double thickness as one stitch. Trim any ends after finishing piece. 83

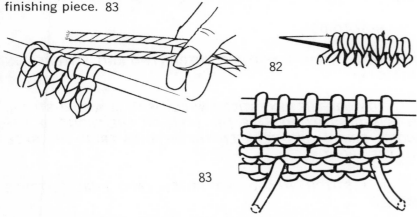

This is very easy for beginners and, with care, can be used at this time. This method is the ideal way of joining mohairs and angora yarns. On ombre (many-colored) yarns be sure that you have the same colors overlapping when joining.

3. SPLICED YARN 84

To splice yarn, about 5" from end of old yarn and new yarn, split, shred or cut out one-half of the thickness. Overlap the ends from both old and new piece, keeping yarn spiraled so this joining will be as smooth as rest of knitting. Trim any ends after piece is finished.

4. YARN THROUGH YARN 85

Thread a blunt yarn sewing needle and run thread through center of old yarn for several inches. Knit through this double thickness and trim ends after piece is finished.

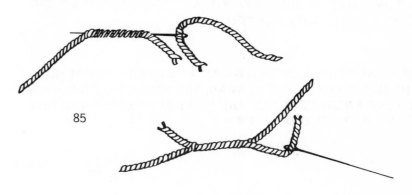

KNOTS

There will be knots in yarns. Don't get upset or angry about them. This is not unusual. In fact, it is quite normal to have a knot or two in a skein of knitting worsted. Some yarns that are difficult to spin may have more. Most yarns have few. The manufacturers are constantly working on this problem and today have almost eliminated knots in yarns.

WHY BE PARTICULAR ABOUT JOINING YARNS?

The manner and place of joining yarns will improve the appearance of your finished garment by 100%. Good joinings will leave no weak places, holes or bumps in the knitting. It certainly is better to have whole pieces of yarn in the garment instead of in a box of left-over yarn.

The improvement proper joinings make in garments is unbelieveable. This was proved over and over in a one-year test in my shop on Ohio State University Campus. Every new knitter was shown where and how to join yarns. Regardless of whether the beginning knitting was fair, good or excellent, sweaters looked lovely and the coeds were delighted because correct joinings allowed garments to be sewed and blocked properly.

IT IS THE "FINISHING" THAT MAKES THE GARMENT. IT IS MOST IMPORTANT THAT YOU REALIZE THE EASE AND QUALITY OF THE SEWING AND FINISHING OF KNITS IS GREATLY DETERMINED BY HOW AND WHERE YARNS ARE JOINED. IF THE SEWING IS EASIER, IT TAKES LESS TIME. THEREFORE, IT IS MORE PRACTICAL, ESPECIALLY IF YOU HAVE TO PAY SOMEONE TO DO THE FINISHING AND SEWING FOR YOU.

THE INSIDE OF A KNITTED GARMENT SHOULD LOOK AS GOOD AS THE OUTSIDE! CAREFUL JOINING AND FINISHING WILL SOON TAKE YOUR KNITTING OUT OF THE "AMATEUR" CLASS AND GIVE YOU THE "PROFESSIONAL LOOK."

R I B B I N G

THUS FAR EACH ROW HAS BEEN MADE USING THE SAME KIND OF STITCH. NOW, WE ARE GOING TO MIX KNIT STITCHES AND PURL STITCHES IN THE SAME ROW.

WHEN, FOR TWO OR MORE ROWS OF ALTERNATING KNITS AND PURLS, KNITS ARE WORKED ON TOP OF KNITS AND PURLS ON TOP OF PURLS, THIS MAKES VERTICAL PATTERNS CALLED "RIBS". THIS PATTERN IS CALLED "RIBBING". 86, 88, 89

On many garments we need a pattern stitch that will pull in, fit snugly, and hold edges in place. Ribbing patterns like *K 1, P 1* or *K 2, P 2* are used to accomplish this. Ribbing, when used on the edges of a knitted item, is usually worked on smaller needles than the rest of the piece.

RIBBING OF K 2, P 2 86

CONTINUING TO WORK ON YOUR 24 STITCHES, THE FIRST RIBBING PATTERN WE WILL MAKE IS ALTERNATING K 2 STITCHES AND P 2 STITCHES, WRITTEN AS FOLLOWS:

RIBBING PATTERN (Multiple of 4)

Row 1: *K 2, P 2, repeat between *'s across row.
Repeat this row for pattern.

HOW TO DO:

*K 1 STITCH, K ANOTHER STITCH (TWO KNIT STITCHES ON NEEDLE).

TO WORK THE NEXT STITCH, WHICH IS TO BE A PURL STITCH, IT IS NECESSARY TO HAVE THE YARN ON THE <u>FRONT</u> OF THE WORK. BRING YARN BETWEEN THE NEEDLES FROM THE BACK TO THE FRONT.

P 1 STITCH, P ANOTHER STITCH (TWO PURL STITCHES MADE).

*PUT YARN BETWEEN THE NEEDLES FROM FRONT TO <u>BACK</u> AND REPEAT BETWEEN *'S ACROSS ROW.*

86

KNIT TIP: WHEN FOLLOWING A KNIT WITH A PURL OR A PURL WITH A KNIT, YARN MUST BE ON CORRECT SIDE OF WORK TO MAKE THAT PARTICULAR STITCH — YARN ON BACK OF WORK FOR KNIT STITCH AND YARN ON FRONT OF WORK FOR PURL STITCH.

KNIT TIP: WHEN PUTTING YARN BACK AND FORTH BETWEEN NEEDLES, DO NOT ALLOW YARN TO BE PLACED OVER TOP OF THE NEEDLE. ANYTIME YOU LAY YARN ACROSS TOP OF NEEDLE YOU WILL GAIN A NEW AND EXTRA STITCH ON NEXT ROW. A HOLE IN THE NEXT ROW WILL THROW OFF THE REGULARITY OF THE RIBBING PATTERN. 87

CHECK YOUR RIBBING AT END OF EACH ROW. ALL ERRORS MUST BE CORRECTED BEFORE YOU CAN WORK NEXT ROW.

DON'T

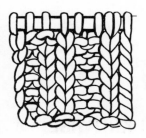
87

Some knitters drop off any extra loops on the next row but this will usually leave a loose place or a hole in the knitting. It is better to undo row and re-knit.

PRACTICE: WORK 6 ROWS OF K 2, P 2, RIBBING ON YOUR 24 STITCHES — WITHOUT MISTAKES!

MAKING RIBBING EASY

THE EASIEST WAY TO LEARN TO DO RIBBING CORRECTLY IS TO REMEMBER THAT THE FIRST ROW OF RIBBING SETS UP THE PATTERN STITCH. (IT DOESN'T MATTER HOW MANY STITCHES, EVEN OR UNEVEN NUMBER).

TURN WORK.

ON THE SECOND AND SUCCEEDING ROWS, DO THE SAME KIND OF STITCH THAT SHOWS OR FACES YOU. KNIT THE KNITS AND PURL THE PURLS.

In this instance, the first two stitches are K 2 sts and P 2 sts and alternate these across row. This pattern contains a repetition or multiple of 4 sts (K 2, P 2) and since 4 divides evenly into 24, you begin each row with the K 2. However, should the number of stitches NOT be divided evenly by the multiple of stitches (4), as K 2, P 2 worked on 26 sts, you must be able to follow the rib stitch without further written instructions. This can be assured in several ways.

1. You can LOOK at the stitch and do the same stitch that shows.

2. You can FOLLOW INSTRUCTIONS in pattern books, which are usually written out row by row.

3. You can be AWARE THAT WHEN YOU HAVE A MULTIPLE PLUS A NUMBER OF STITCHES, EVERY ROW WILL NOT NECESSARILY BEGIN WITH THE SAME KIND OF STITCH.

This points out an instance where a basic knowledge of knitting instructions is expected by the companies putting out pattern books. Many patterns will merely instruct you to do ribbing of K 2, P 2 for so many rows or inches on so many stitches.

YOU ARE RESPONSIBLE FOR KEEPING IN PATTERN, REGARDLESS OF THE NUMBER OF STITCHES.

RIBBING OF K 3, P 3   88

PRACTICE: ON THE 24 STITCHES, WORK 6 ROWS OF THE FOLLOWING:

RIBBING PATTERN (Multiple of 6)

*K 3, P 3, repeat between *'s across row.
Repeat this row for pattern.

88

RIBBING OF K 1, P 1 89

PRACTICE: ON THE 24 STITCHES, WORK 6 ROWS OF THE FOLLOWING:

RIBBING PATTERN (Multiple of 2)

*K 1, P 1, repeat between *'s across row.
Repeat this row for pattern.

89

A SLIP STITCH

A SLIP STITCH IS A STITCH TRANSFERRED FROM ONE NEEDLE TO ANOTHER WITHOUT WORKING IT.

KNIT TIP: ALWAYS SLIP STITCHES PURLWISE, UNLESS INSTRUCTIONS TELL YOU OTHERWISE.

This allows slip stitch to lay in the same direction on needle as other stitches (right side of loop on top of needle) and slip stitches will work off flat on next row with no twists or errors.

THE KIND OF STITCH, WHETHER KNIT OR PURL, DOES NOT ALTER THE MANNER OF SLIPPING THE STITCH.

TO SLIP A STITCH PURLWISE 90

INSERT RIGHT NEEDLE IN RIGHT SIDE OF FIRST STITCH ON LEFT NEEDLE AS IF YOU ARE GOING TO PURL A STITCH. SLIP THIS LOOP FROM LEFT NEEDLE TO RIGHT NEEDLE. ONE STITCH HAS BEEN SLIPPED. THE SAME MOTIONS, IN REVERSE, ARE USED TO SLIP FROM RIGHT NEEDLE TO LEFT NEEDLE.

90

TO SLIP A STITCH KNITWISE 91

INSERT NEEDLE LIKE A KNIT STITCH AND SLIP OFF LEFT NEEDLE TO RIGHT NEEDLE.

91

This slip stitch lays on the needle with the <u>LEFT</u> side of loop on top or contrary to the rest of the stitches.

Slipping knitwise will be used later in decreasing, shaping and in lace knitting.

SLIP STITCH USED FOR TURNING VERTICAL EDGES

The pattern K 1, S1 1, K 1 is the basis for turning vertical edges on facings of coats and sweaters.

What happens is this: Actually the slip stitch is worked only every other row. When you slip a stitch, it is not worked and therefore does not have the thickness of a full stitch. On the next row this stitch is purled and slip stitch is then spread two rows in height. When repeating these two rows, the slip stitch on one row and purling on the next, this one stitch will be thinner and makes an excellent folding line on the knitting with the slip stitch becoming the edge of the piece. 92 93

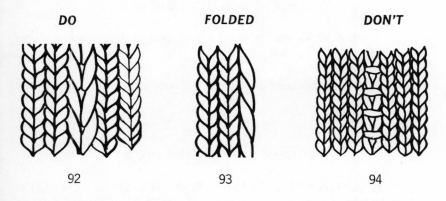

DO	FOLDED	DON'T
92	93	94

POSITION OF YARN FOR SLIP STITCH

The most common error beginners make in slipping stitches is the belief that to slip purlwise, it is necessary to have the yarn at the front of the work. This in incorrect.

If instructions say " K 1, S1 1, K 1", leave yarn at BACK of work before slipping. Do NOT bring yarn to front of work before slipping. This error is very unfortunate, for the edges will NOT fold back flat but puff out and not block evenly. The purpose of the slip stitch has been completely lost — plus another problem has been made on the edges. 94

If instructions say "P 1, S1 1, P 1", leave yarn on FRONT of work. Do not put yarn to back of work.

If instructions say " K 1, bring yarn forward, S1 1, put yarn back between needles, K 1", these are specific instructions for special patterns, like fabric stitch, and should be followed exactly.

BINDING OFF

BINDING OFF, SOMETIMES CALLED "CASTING OFF", IS FASTENING STITCHES TO MAKE AN EDGE. THIS CAN BE DONE IN KNIT, PURL OR PATTERN STITCH.

KNIT TIP: WITH FEW EXCEPTIONS, BINDING OFF IS DONE ONLY AT THE BEGINNING OF A ROW.

BIND OFF METHOD NO. 1

I USE THIS METHOD EXCLUSIVELY. IT WILL GIVE YOU THE SMOOTHEST, MOST ELASTIC EDGE AND WILL WORK OFF BEST, TO GIVE THE SAME SIZE AND STRETCH AS REST OF KNITTING.

BINDING OFF KNITWISE

*KNIT UNTIL 2 STITCHES ARE ON RIGHT NEEDLE.

TAKE LEFT NEEDLE, INSERT NEEDLE IN LEFT FRONT OF THE FIRST STITCH MADE ON RIGHT HAND NEEDLE. 95

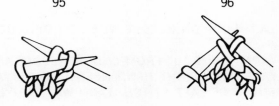

95　　　　　96

LIFT THIS LOOP UP AND OVER THE SECOND STITCH MADE AND DROP OFF TIP OF RIGHT HAND NEEDLE. ONE STITCH HAS BEEN BOUND OFF. 96

KNIT TIP: YOU HAVE BOUND OFF ONE STITCH. ONE LOOP IS LEFT ON RIGHT HAND NEEDLE. DO NOT WORK TWO MORE STITCHES, BUT ONLY ONE MORE. INSTRUCTIONS SAY, "KNIT UNTIL 2 STITCHES ARE ON RIGHT HAND NEEDLE."

*REPEAT FROM * UNTIL THE CORRECT NUMBER OF STITCHES HAVE BEEN BOUND OFF OR ONLY ONE LOOP REMAINS ON RIGHT NEEDLE.*

PLEASE NOTE THAT YOU DO NOT COUNT A STITCH AS "BOUND-OFF" UNTIL YOU HAVE LIFTED ONE LOOP OVER AND OFF ANOTHER.

BINDING OFF PURLWISE

*P 2 STITCHES TO RIGHT HAND NEEDLE.

*WORKING FROM EITHER THE BACK OR FRONT OF WORK, LIFT FIRST PURL STITCH MADE OVER SECOND STITCH AND DROP OFF END OF RIGHT NEEDLE, 97 AS YOU DID FOR KNIT STITCH. REPEAT BETWEEN *'S AS OFTEN AS NEEDED.*

KNIT TIP: REMEMBER THAT THERE ARE ONLY 2 STITCHES ON RIGHT HAND NEEDLE AT ONE TIME FOR BINDING OFF.

LAST LOOP ON NEEDLE WHEN BINDING OFF

CUT YARN ABOUT 10" FROM END OF NEEDLE AND PULL UP LOOP OF YARN WITH RIGHT HAND NEEDLE UNTIL YARN COMES OUT OF CENTER OF LAST STITCH. YARN WILL NOT UNRAVEL. 98

DO   **DON'T**

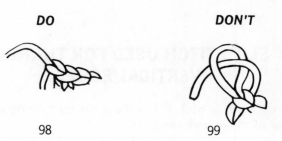

98   99

DO NOT PULL END OF YARN THROUGH LAST LOOP ON NEEDLE. (99) This makes knots and lumps in knitted pieces. Many times to finish garments properly, these knots have to be removed. This work is time consuming, costly, sometimes difficult to do, irritating and unnecessary if knitter would just think a little as to what she is trying to accomplish at this point.

BINDING OFF TOO TIGHTLY

1. In right hand, use a needle one, two or three sizes larger for binding off.

2. Or, loosen tension of yarn when wrapping.

BINDING OFF METHOD NO. 2

** K 2 STITCHES TOGETHER. SLIP THIS STITCH ON LEFT HAND NEEDLE. REPEAT BETWEEN *'S UNTIL ALL STITCHES HAVE BEEN BOUND OFF.*

100

This is a very tight, rigid edge but could be useful in the proper place.

INCREASES

TO INCREASE IS TO MAKE MORE.

More stitches will make the knitting WIDER. Increases can be made anywhere in the knitting but are usually worked on the knit side of the garment.

The type of increase used is determined by the pattern stitch and place it is used in the knitting. It may be smooth, rough, tight, loose, lean to the right or lean to the left. It is best to learn the basic types of increases and then use the one that will be most suitable and look the best at that particular spot. Several different types of increases may be used on the same garment.

METHOD NO. 1 INCREASE — KNITWISE
(Two stitches made from one)

KNIT IN THE FRONT AND BACK OF STITCH AS FOLLOWS:

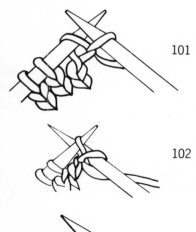

101

KNIT THE STITCH BUT DO NOT PULL OFF OLD STITCH. 101

102

PLACE INDEX FINGER ON TOP OF FIRST LOOP ON RIGHT HAND NEEDLE. BRING TIP OF RIGHT HAND NEEDLE TO THE RIGHT, AROUND AND BACK OF LEFT NEEDLE. INSERT RIGHT NEEDLE IN BACK LOOP OF THIS SAME STITCH. 102

103

KNIT THIS BACK LOOP, PULLING NEW STITCH OUT IN EXACTLY THE SAME PLACE AS NEEDLE WAS INSERTED. THERE ARE TWO LOOPS ON RIGHT NEEDLE. 103

104

PULL OFF 2 STITCHES. 104

This increase is very easy to do and is probably the most frequently used. However, it is not recommended for use in stockinette stitch pattern, except on the edges, since the small "nub" in the increase, which looks like a purl stitch, will interrupt the pattern and look like an error in the knitting.

You can also do this increase, as in Continental knitting, first knitting in the back of the stitch and then in the front.

METHOD NO. 1 INCREASE — PURLWISE
(Two stitches made from one)

PURL IN THE FRONT AND BACK OF STITCH AS FOLLOWS:

105

PURL THE FIRST STITCH BUT DO NOT PULL OFF. 105

106

PLACE INDEX FINGER ON TOP OF FIRST LOOP ON RIGHT HAND NEEDLE. BRING TIP OF RIGHT HAND NEEDLE AROUND TO BACK OF LEFT NEEDLE. INSTEAD OF INSERTING NEEDLE STRAIGHT IN BACK LOOP AS

107

ON KNIT INCREASE, CONTINUE AROUND THE BACK OF STITCH, TO THE FAR SIDE, AND INSERT IN LEFT SIDE OF BACK LOOP. 106 *BRING NEEDLE TO FRONT AND WORK LIKE A REGULAR PURL STITCH.*

PULL 2 STITCHES OFF. 107

This is particularly useful when it is necessary to increase purl stitches in ribbing.

METHOD NO. 2 INCREASE
(One stitch increased on Stockinette stitch by picking up to right and left of stitch)

TO MAKE INCREASE LEANING TO RIGHT OF STITCH:

108   109

WORK UP TO THE STITCH WHERE INCREASE IS TO BE MADE.

FROM THE FRONT OF WORK INSERT RIGHT HAND NEEDLE IN RIGHT SIDE OF FIRST LOOP UNDER FIRST STITCH ON LEFT HAND NEEDLE. 108

KNIT THIS LOOP. 109 **INCREASE WHICH HAS BEEN MADE, LEANS TO THE RIGHT. KNIT THE NEXT STITCH AND CONTINUE IN PATTERN.**

TO MAKE INCREASE LEANING TO LEFT OF STITCH:

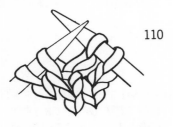 110

111

KNIT THE STITCH UNDER WHICH THE INCREASE IS TO BE MADE.

INSERT LEFT HAND NEEDLE FROM THE BACK OF WORK INTO THE SECOND LOOP BELOW THE KNIT ON RIGHT NEEDLE. 110

KNIT THE LOOP. 111 **INCREASE HAS BEEN MADE, LEANS TO LEFT. CONTINUE IN PATTERN.**

I do not believe this increase is easy to do well. It does not lay as flat as other increases and has a tendency to pucker a little. This increase is often used when knitting skirts from the top down, which gives you more control over the length of the skirt. However, it is usually easier for most knitters to work skirts from the bottom up since decreases are easier to make than increases.

METHOD NO. 3 INCREASE — KNITWISE
(One stitch in Stockinette Stitch made on bar between stitches)

WITH RIGHT NEEDLE AND FROM BACK, PICK UP BAR, ALSO CALLED "RUNNING THREAD", BEFORE NEXT STITCH. 112 **PLACE LOOP ON LEFT NEEDLE WITH THE RIGHT SIDE OF THE LOOP ON TOP.** 113

112

KNIT IN THE BACK OF THIS LOOP. PULL OFF STITCH. 114

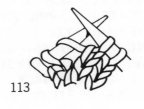

113

NOTE THAT STITCH IS TWISTED. THIS IS CORRECT.
115

114   115

If it is difficult to directly insert needle in back of the stitch, first insert needle in front and roll over top of left needle to back. Then knit loop.

This increase actually twists the stitch and fills in beautifully and smoothly. If bar was knitted from front and NOT twisted, it would leave a hole on next row. This is done on certain pattern stitches, but is not correct for this increase.

This increase is the most satisfactory on flat knitting and is the one I use 99% of the time. It is especially effective placed two or three stitches in from edges of pieces, thus allowing straight edges for easy-to-do and neat seam sewing. This increase is least noticeable in the body of garments.

METHOD NO. 3 INCREASE — PURLWISE
(One stitch on Stockinette stitch, purl side, made on bar between stitches)

PICK UP BAR, OR "RUNNING THREAD", BEFORE NEXT STITCH. PLACE LOOP ON LEFT NEEDLE WITH THE LEFT SIDE OF LOOP ON TOP OF NEEDLE. 116 NOTE THIS IS CONTRARY TO THE USUAL MANNER.

116

117

PURL IN REGULAR FASHION. 117

Again you have twisted the increase stitch which fills in beautifully. Seldom is it necessary to do this purlwise.

METHOD NO. 4 INCREASE
(Adding stitches at beginning and end of rows)

1. Increase by casting on loops as in Method No. 1. (Page 12)
2. Increase by knitting on loops as in Method No. 2 (Page 50)
3. Increase by knitting on loops as in Method No. 3 (Page 51), using an extra or "free" needle, then working these stitches onto the other needle.

METHOD NO. 5 INCREASE
YARN OVERS
(Illustrated on Stockinette stitch)

A YARN OVER (YO) IS A NEW STITCH MADE BY LAYING YARN ACROSS TOP OF RIGHT NEEDLE.

A YARN OVER WILL LAY IN THE SAME DIRECTION AS OTHER STITCHES ON NEEDLE, WITH RIGHT SIDE OF LOOP ON TOP.

A YARN OVER WILL BE WORKED AS A STITCH ON THE NEXT ROW AND IT WILL LEAVE A HOLE, SOMETIMES CALLED AN "EYELET", UNDER THE YARN OVER.

THE SECRET OF MAKING YO'S

THE KIND OF STITCH, KNIT OR PURL, THAT FOLLOWS THE YO DETERMINES THE MANNER IN WHICH THE YARN IS WRAPPED AROUND THE RIGHT NEEDLE. THE YO DOES NOT COMPLETE ITSELF UNTIL THE NEXT STITCH IS MADE.

BASIC YO COMBINATIONS

K 1, YO, K 1

K 1 STITCH. 118

YO BY BRINGING YARN BETWEEN NEEDLES AS IF YOU ARE GOING TO PURL.

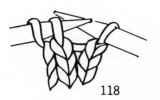
118

119

REPLACE RIGHT HAND ON NEEDLE, WHICH WILL LAY YARN ACROSS TOP OF RIGHT NEEDLE. 119

KNIT NEXT STITCH, WHICH ALLOWS THREAD TO CONTINUE AROUND RIGHT NEEDLE (COUNTERCLOCKWISE). 120,121

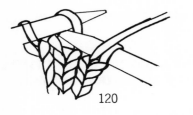

120

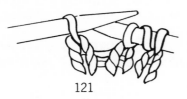

121

K 1, YO, P 1

K 1 STITCH. BRING YARN BETWEEN NEEDLES AS IF YOU ARE GOING TO PURL. 122,123

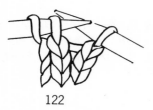

122

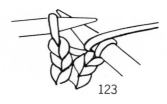

123

THEN CONTINUE TO WRAP ENTIRELY AROUND RIGHT NEEDLE AGAIN (COUNTERCLOCKWISE) ENDING ON THE FRONT OF WORK. 124 P 1. 125

124

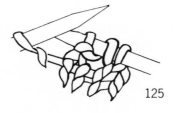

125

PLEASE CHECK THIS: IF YOU DO NOT HAVE A YO HERE, YOU HAVE NEGLECTED, AFTER BRINGING YARN TO FRONT OF WORK, TO CONTINUE TO WRAP YARN ENTIRELY AROUND NEEDLE, ENDING ON FRONT. RIGHT NEEDLE HAS A COMPLETE LOOP FOR THIS YO WHICH LAYS IN SAME DIRECTION ON THE NEEDLE AS REST OF STITCHES.

P 1, YO, P 1

P 1. 126 WRAP YARN ENTIRELY AROUND NEEDLE (COUNTER-CLOCKWISE). 127 P 1. 128

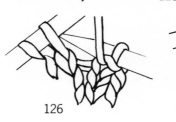

126

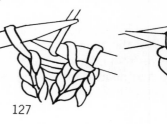

127

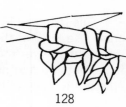

128

P 1, YO, K 1

P 1. 129 LEAVE YARN AT FRONT OF WORK. 130 K 1. 131

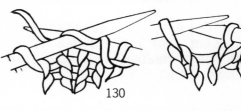

129

130

131

BY LEAVING YARN AT FRONT OF WORK, WHEN STITCH IS KNITTED, THREAD IS AUTOMATICALLY LAID ACROSS TOP OF NEEDLE.

METHOD NO. 6 INCREASE (EYELET)

The English "make one" is made by knitting under the bar between two stitches 132 , which makes a hole on the next row. 133

132

133

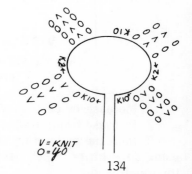

134

SOME USES FOR YO'S

1. Used for increases, as in raglan sleeved garments. 134
Example: In a basic raglan sweater with YO increases, called an "open" or "lace" raglan, the seam stitch and Yo increases often are written as follows: Row 1: (Right Front) K 10, *Yo, K 1, Yo, * (Sleeve) K 2, repeat between the first two *'s, (Back) K 10, repeat between the first two *'s, (sleeve), K 2, repeat between the first two *'s, (Left Front) K 10.

2. For lace patterns where the number of stitches remains the same in each row, these Yo's are extra stitches. Therefore, an equal number of stitches are decreased in the row to take care of these extra stitches. A good example of this is the Feather and Fan pattern on Page 69.

3. For beadings (holes to run ribbons or cords through), Yo's are made about every 3rd stitch as follows: *K 1, YO, K 2 tog., repeat between *'s across row. 135 This is often used in baby booties, necks of sweaters and trimmings.

4. For picot edges, these Yo's are made across a row in the same manner as for beading, alternating knits and Yo's every second, third or fourth stitches. 135. When piece is finished, it is folded along row of Yo's to make the picot edge. 136

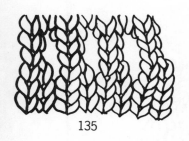

135

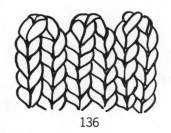

136

5. For Lacy Rib pattern, when combining Yo's and other stitches, such as *K 1, Yo, S1 1 (as if to purl), K 2 tog., * the basic rule still holds true. The knit or purl stitch FOLLOWING the Yo determines how the Yo is made. The basic principals here would be K, YO, K.

DECREASES

TO DECREASE MEANS TO MAKE LESS.

Fewer stitches will make piece more narrow. Decreases can be made anywhere in the knitting and are usually made on the knit side of the garment.

WORKING STITCHES TOGETHER

TO DECREASE ONE STITCH AT A TIME

K 2 stitches together 137 or P 2 stitches together 138 — written K 2 tog. or P 2 tog. Looking at knit side of piece, the K 2 tog. leans to right.

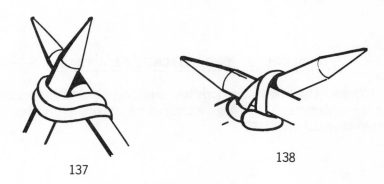

137   138

PASS SLIP STITCH OVER (PSSO) OR SLIP, KNIT AND PASS (SKP)

FOR THIS DECREASING ONLY, THE SLIP STITCH, WHEN DONE ON A KNIT ROW, SHOULD ALWAYS BE SLIPPED KNITWISE SO SLIP STITCH PASSED OVER WILL LAY IN A FLAT, NOT A TWISTED, LOOP.

TO DECREASE ONE STITCH AT A TIME

Slip one stitch knitwise, knit one stitch, pass the slip stitch over and off end of needle (same as binding off). Note decrease leans to left. 139, 140, 141

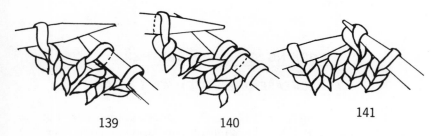

139   140   141

These instructions would be written, "Sl 1, K 1, PSSO", or "SKP".

TO DECREASE TWO STITCHES AT A TIME

Slip one stitch knitwise, knit two together, pass the slip stitch over — written "Sl 1, K 2 tog., PSSO". This makes a "cluster" as used in lace patterns. 142

142

MATCHING DECREASES

Please note in making decreases that some decreased stitches lean to the right and some to the left. Some are worked firmly, some are the same size as the regularly worked stitches and some are loose.

Yarn companies do not and will not take the time or space to write out and explain the technique of matching decreases, when it is clear and easy to write the most commonly used shaping which is as follows:

"K 2, Sl 1, K 1, PSSO, K across row to last 4 sts, K 2 tog., K 2." These two decreases do not match! However, the finished sewed seams will look alike. 143.

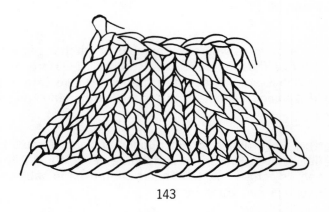

143

Following are listed the exact matches for basic decreases. The decrease is usually selected that leans in the SAME direction as the knitting is being shaped. On full-fashioned sleeves, where the decrease is done several stitches in from edge to show as a trim, it often goes AGAINST the shaping. 144

144

DECREASE TO MATCH K 2 TOGETHER (149)

LEFT EDGE OF KNITTING (K 2 tog. slants to right) 149

WORK UP TO THE TWO STITCHES TO BE USED FOR DECREASE.

1. K 2 TOG.

145

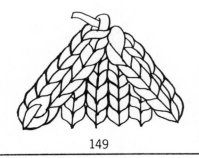

149

RIGHT EDGE OF KNITTING (K 2 tog. slants to left) 149

WORK UP TO THE TWO STITCHES TO BE USED FOR DECREASE.

1. SI 1 st KNITWISE (2 times). This will place LEFT side of loops on top of needle. 146
2. AT BACK of work, insert left needle straight through the center of these two stitches. 147
3. K 2 tog. 148

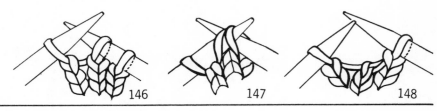

146   147   148

DECREASE TO MATCH SL 1, K 1, PSSO (157)

LEFT EDGE OF KNITTING (Slants right) 157

WORK UP TO THE TWO STITCHES TO BE USED FOR DECREASE.

1. K 1 150
2. SI (PURLWISE) this stitch back to left needle. 151
3. Pass the second stitch on left needle over the first stitch (already knitted) and off the end of needle. 152
4. SI (PURLWISE) the first stitch on left needle to right needle. 153

150

152

151

153

RIGHT EDGE OF KNITTING (Slants left) 157

WORK UP TO THE TWO STITCHES TO BE USED FOR DECREASE.

1. SI 1 st (KNITWISE). 154
2. K 1 st.
3. Insert left needle on front in slip stitch made on right needle, and pass slip stitch over and off end of needle of work. 155, 156

154

155

156

157

These matching slip stitch decreases are loops that have not been worked so they will be bigger and looser than the decreases made by working two stitches together. This decrease is more effective and decorative on the third and fourth stitches from edges and will allow straight edges for neat seam sewing.

CONTINENTAL KNITTING

This is also sometimes called Italian, German, European, "pick" or crochet knitting.

CASTING ON

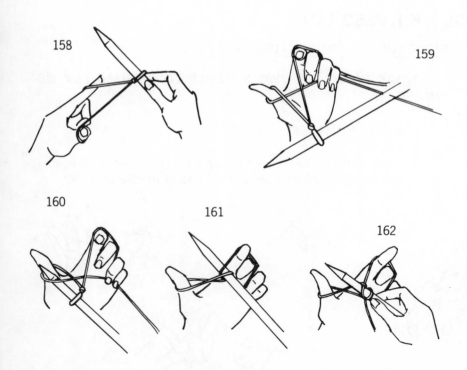

CONTINENTAL KNITTING WITH LEFT SIDE OF LOOP ON FRONT OF NEEDLE

KNIT STITCH   *PURL STITCH*

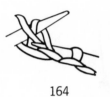

163   164

CONTINENTAL KNITTING WITH THE RIGHT SIDE OF LOOP ON FRONT OF NEEDLE

KNIT STITCH   *PURL STITCH*

165   166

HAVE YOU NOTICED THAT YOU HAVE BEEN READING INSTRUCTIONS?

It is really very painless. So many knitters say they can do the stitches but cannot read instructions.

This "knitting language" is quickly learned and reading instructions becomes quite easy. The abbreviations, special terms, symbols and definitions will seem strange only a short time since most pattern books list this information.

FIRST, READ ALL THE INSTRUCTIONS FOR THE PIECE OR SECTION YOU ARE MAKING, AS FOR A SLEEVE. THEN BEGIN AGAIN AND READ THE FIRST SENTENCE AND WORK INSTRUCTIONS AS GIVEN IN THAT SENTENCE. CONTINUE SENTENCE BY SENTENCE.

MANY BEGINNERS READ TOO MUCH OR TOO LITTLE. DO NOT STOP AT COMMAS WHEN READING, FOR THE INSTRUCTIONS MAY MEAN SOMETHING ENTIRELY DIFFERENT WHEN THE ENTIRE SENTENCE HAS BEEN READ. DO STOP AT SEMI-COLONS.

Different designers, companies and countries write and set up instructions in different forms and sequences — but achieve the same results. Most yarn companies try to be very explicit but each company's designer or fashion editor has her favorite way of writing instructions. You will soon become accustomed to the writing manner of each company, much as you do in using sewing patterns from different companies.

All yarn companies endeavor to write clear, concise instructions. but it is also necessary for the companies to be practical and to consolidate and simplify, to eliminate excessive printing and packaging costs. Therefore, if you say, "Why don't they tell me how?", or "Why don't they write this out?", it is usually a "basic" technique of knitting you are expected to know.

KNIT TIP: WHEN YOU PURCHASE PATTERN BOOKS FOR KNITS, THEY ARE NOT MANUALS FOR TEACHING KNITTING, BUT PATTERNS WITH DIRECTIONS FOR MAKING GARMENTS AND IT IS "UNDERSTOOD" AND "EXPECTED" THAT YOU KNOW THE BASICS OF KNITTING: HOW TO KNIT, PURL, CAST ON, BIND OFF, INCREASE, DECREASE, ETC.

ERRORS IN PATTERNS

Once in awhile there will be an error in knitting books. The error will probably be discovered after you have done some knitting and find pattern doesn't work out right. Do not be too disturbed and unforgiving towards the company. These patterns are worked out by PEOPLE — designers, knitters, typists, and printers — who are just as sorry as you, that this error occurred. Every effort is made to make accurate pattern instructions and to print correctly.

For the very critical, try designing and writing pattern instructions in all sizes for commercial use, for which you will be responsible. It is a difficult and exacting occupation. It is so easy to make a mistake and fail to catch the error. Considering the thousands of patterns available, I am always amazed there aren't more errors.

However, when you do find a "real" error, your yarn shop or department store will appreciate learning about it. If they are unaware of it, you will be doing a good deed by keeping other knitters from making the same mistake.

Although yarn companies are not liable for variations of individual knitters or for human or typographical errors, a few of them will send correction sheets for inserting in their pattern books. This is very helpful, much appreciated, but rarely done.

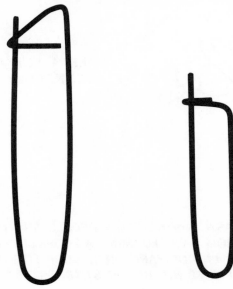

OTHER METHODS OF CASTING ON STITCHES

Let's talk a little about casting on. Do be very particular about cast-on rows. Do not use yarn on this row that contains any knots or defects. Use single yarn for casting on, except possibly for a lightly spun yarn like mohair, that pulls apart easily. On the bottom edges of boys' and men's sweaters that would get very hard wear, sometimes double thicknesses of yarn are used.

THERE ARE MANY AND VARIOUS COMBINATIONS FOR CASTING ON STITCHES BUT THE THREE METHODS LISTED ARE BASIC.

METHOD NO. 1 — KNITWISE

See page 12.

METHOD NO. 1 — PURLWISE 167

167

MAKE A SLIP LOOP AND PLACE NEEDLE IN RIGHT HAND.

***PICK UP YARN COMING FROM NEEDLE AND LAY ACROSS YARN COMING FROM BALL, FORMING A LOOP. SLIP LOOP ONTO NEEDLE, PULLING END OF YARN UNTIL LOOP FITS. REPEAT BETWEEN*'S FOR DESIRED NUMBER OF STITCHES.**

METHOD NO. 2 — KNITWISE 168, 169, 170

WORKING WITH TWO NEEDLES, MAKE A SLIP LOOP ON ONE NEEDLE ABOUT 6" FROM END OF YARN. PLACE NEEDLE IN LEFT HAND.

***WITH SECOND NEEDLE IN RIGHT HAND, K 1 STITCH IN THIS LOOP AND REPLACE THIS KNIT STITCH ONTO LEFT NEEDLE. REPEAT BETWEEN *'S UNTIL DESIRED NUMBER OF LOOPS HAVE BEEN CAST ON.**

168   169   170

I seldom use this method. It usually gives a tight and ungiving edge. If cast on loosely, it gives a very poor, lacy and loose edge. A garment with this kind of edge does not meet my standards for assembling and finishing. I am never pleased with the results.

However, you will find this method in several beginners' books because it is easy to do, easy to illustrate, easy to write the instructions and while casting on stitch, you learn to make the knit stitch.

An interesting edge for socks is to use Method No. 2 of casting on but instead of knitting IN the stitch, knit BETWEEN the stitches. This allows a good edge because it is double yet flexible. Watch this method — not too tight or too loose!

METHOD NO. 3 — KNITWISE
(Knitting on)

THIS METHOD IS THE MOST USEFUL AND MOST SATISFACTORY. IT WILL GIVE YOU A STRONG, FLEXIBLE DOUBLE EDGE, WHICH CAN BE CAST ON KNITWISE, PURLWISE OR IN PATTERN. THIS IS SOMETIMES CALLED "DOUBLE CASTING ON" BUT DOES NOT MEAN THAT DOUBLE STRANDS OF YARN ARE USED.

WHEN USING KNITTING WORSTED, MEASURE OFF ABOUT 1" OF YARN FOR EACH STITCH TO BE CAST ON AND MAKE A SLIP LOOP ON NEEDLE. PLACE NEEDLE IN RIGHT HAND.

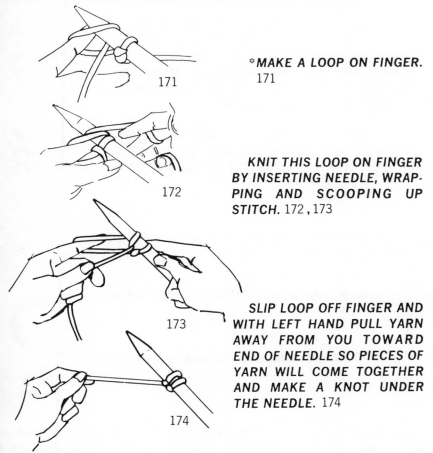

*MAKE A LOOP ON FINGER.
171

KNIT THIS LOOP ON FINGER BY INSERTING NEEDLE, WRAPPING AND SCOOPING UP STITCH. 172, 173

SLIP LOOP OFF FINGER AND WITH LEFT HAND PULL YARN AWAY FROM YOU TOWARD END OF NEEDLE SO PIECES OF YARN WILL COME TOGETHER AND MAKE A KNOT UNDER THE NEEDLE. 174

REPEAT BETWEEN *'S UNTIL REQUIRED NUMBER OF STITCHES ARE ON NEEDLE.

If yarn spreads under needle, you are pulling yarn sideways, or yarn in right hand is not keeping proper tension.

If stitches pile up, pull AWAY from you toward end of needle.

If stitches are too tight, ease the tension of the thread in right hand just as the yarns meet to make a knot under needle.

The more practice and experience in knitting, the nicer the cast-on edge will be.

For facings and pieces made in Stockinette stitch, this cast-on row is Row 1 or the Knit row.

METHOD NO. 3 — PURLWISE
(Purling on)

ALLOWING ABOUT 1" OF YARN FOR EACH STITCH TO BE CAST ON, MEASURE OFF SUFFICIENT YARN FOR NUMBER OF STITCHES REQUIRED.

MAKE SLIP LOOP AND PLACE NEEDLE IN RIGHT HAND.

*MAKE A LOOP ON LEFT INDEX FINGER. BE SURE TO BRING YARN TO FRONT OF WORK (BETWEEN NEEDLE AND LOOP ON FINGER). IT WILL REMAIN ON FRONT OF WORK FOR PURLING.

INSERT NEEDLE IN RIGHT FRONT OF LOOP AND DO NOT SLIP YARN OFF FINGER. PURL THIS LOOP BY WRAPPING NEEDLE WITH YARN, PUSHING OUT STITCH, SLIPPING OFF FINGER AND WITH LEFT HAND, PULLING YARN AWAY FROM YOU TOWARD END OF NEEDLE SO THAT YARN WILL COME TOGETHER AND MAKE A KNOT UNDER THE NEEDLE. 175, 176

REPEAT BETWEEN *'S UNTIL STITCHES ARE CAST ON NEEDLE.

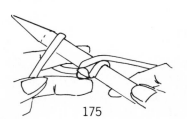

51

As you cast on, left hand will have an open loop which looks very peculiar but this is correct and will give proper results.

If you are starting a knitted piece in Stockinette stitch, as for hems and facings, cast on purls will eliminate a ridge on the right side of your cast-on row and will allow you to work Row 1 in a knit stitch.

177

METHOD NO. 3 — IN PATTERN

WITH A LITTLE PREPARATION, YOU CAN CAST ON STITCHES IN PATTERN, USING ANY COMBINATION OF KNITS AND PURLS.

KNITTING NEEDLES AND ACCESSORIES

Since the sizes of the knitting needles used in this book are some of those most often used, space will not be alloted to the discussion of knitting needles. However, there are several knitting accessories that are quite helpful.

ROW COUNTER 177

A ROW COUNTER IS A KNITTING GADGET THAT HAS TWO DIALS WHICH YOU TURN, BY HAND, AT THE END OF EACH ROW WORKED, TO KEEP COUNT OF THE ROWS. THIS CAN BE PLACED ON A KNITTING NEEDLE FOR SAFE KEEPING AND EASY USE.

KNIT TIP: IT IS IMPORTANT THAT YOU REMEMBER TO TURN ROW COUNTER AT END OF EACH ROW WORKED. WHEN YOU RESUME KNITTING, THE NUMBER SHOWING ON ROW COUNTER IS THE NUMBER OF THE ROW YOU WILL BEGIN OR YOU ARE IN THE MIDDLE OF. ONLY "PRESENT" OR "FUTURE" NUMBER OF ROW SHOULD BE INDICATED.

STITCH HOLDERS 178

STITCH HOLDERS ARE LIKE BIG, BLUNT-END SAFETY PINS, TO HOLD STITCHES THAT YOU WISH TO PUT OUT OF WORK FOR LATER USE. Example: Pocket linings, neck edges, sections of a raglan sweater, tops of shoulders, etc.

TO USE STITCH HOLDER, TAKE IN RIGHT HAND AND SLIP THE STITCHES FROM NEEDLE ONE BY ONE TO HOLDER. FASTEN HOLDER. IF YARN IS TO BE CUT, LEAVE A GOOD END, ABOUT 12".

NEVER, NEVER, NEVER, USE SAFETY PINS FOR STITCH HOLDERS!

178

Some patterns have recommended that stitches be taken off on a string. I do not recommend this, for the stitches are difficult to handle and to pick up again on needles. An exception to this would be when it is necessary to try on a circular knitted skirt.

STITCH MARKERS 179

COMMERCIAL STITCH MARKERS ARE MANUFACTURED RINGS WHICH COME IN VARIOUS COLORS, SIZES AND MATERIALS WITH OPEN OR CLOSED RINGS. THESE ARE EXCELLENT AIDS.

Be sure that you use open rings if markers are to be left in the garment, as for marking increases in knitted skirts. Closed rings would have to be cut out and this is not only dangerous but difficult to do without cutting the yarn.

Guard against using too large markers and for too long a time, because yarn can be marked.

Useful markers may be a small length of thread, yarn or string.

NEVER, NEVER, NEVER, USE SAFETY PINS FOR MARKERS!

HOW TO MARK STITCHES

1. For a stationary marker, place marker through stitch and let it remain. Example: "Mark beginning of row to indicate where armhole shaping begins."

2. For a moving marker, marker is usually placed on right needle immediately before the stitch to be marked. On the following rows when marker is reached, slip marker from left needle to right needle on every row. Example: "Work to marker, slip marker, K 1, etc." This is particularly useful when making seamless raglan sweaters.

HOW TO MARK ROWS

1. Place marker in edge of row.

2. Knit a piece of fine thread, string or yarn along with yarn for several stitches across row. This extra thread is easily removed when garment is finished.

KNIT TIP: BEWARE OF USING A COLOR OF THREAD, STRING OR YARN MATERIAL THAT WILL MARK OR COLOR YOUR KNITTING, LIKE RED ON WHITE YARN.

HOW TO MAKE VERTICAL MARKERS

1. Mark one stitch with a piece of thread, so verticle measuring can be done, as for measuring armholes.

2. Place a piece of yarn or string between the stitches to be marked and each time it is reached in working a row, move piece for marker from front to back.

SEWING NEEDLES FOR YARN 180

NEEDLES FOR SEWING YARN ARE BLUNT END AND HAVE LARGE EYES.

The metal needles come in two sizes, the small size for yarns through 4 ply size and the large size for quick knit and bulky yarns.

The plastic yarn needle comes in one size and is excellent for nubby and "thick and thin" yarns.

Darning needles or sharp pointed needles are very bad for sewing yarn since they will split and tear the yarn in sewing.

180

HOW TO "CHANGE NEEDLES"

WHEN KNITTING INSTRUCTIONS TELL YOU TO CHANGE FROM ONE PAIR OF NEEDLES TO A DIFFERENT SIZE, ON THE SAME PIECE OF KNITTING, THIS MEANS TO WORK THE NEXT TWO ROWS WITH THE NEW SIZE NEEDLES,

Example: When changing from No. 4 to No. 8 needles, your knitted piece will probably be on one No. 4 needle. Put down the free No. 4 needle. Pick up a No. 8 needle and work across one row. This frees the second No. 4 needle. Now pick up second No. 8 needle and work across row. You have changed to a different sized pair of needles. This procedure also applies to changing from large to small needles.

DON'T PULL NEEDLES OUT OF YARN TO CHANGE NEEDLES. ALWAYS KEEP ALL LOOPS ON NEEDLES.

Some knitters take the instructions literally and pull needle out of knitting, leaving the loops loose, and then try to pick up the loops with the new size needle. This is unnecessary, hazardous and difficult.

However, if you have been unfortunate enough to misunderstand the instructions, don't try to pick up small loops or stitches with a large needle. Pick up with a smaller needle, beginning at end of row opposite from where knitting will begin. Then work with the correct size needle in pattern.

PREPARING YARNS FOR REKNITTING

There will be times when you will have to unravel knitting, wish to reknit or design a garment from the used yarn. You will find the yarn, especially after having been blocked, has kinks, twists, etc.

KNIT TIP: YARN WILL NOT REKNIT SMOOTHLY WITHOUT THE KINKS BEING REMOVED. BLOCKING WILL NOT REMOVE THE KINKS.

The easiest and best way to prepare yarn is to make into hanks or skeins by winding yarn around and around, over the thumb and under the elbow. Using a contrasting color of yarn or string, tie easily in two places through center of hank, so yarn will be like a ring.

181

DO NOT PUT MORE THAN 2 OZ. OF YARN OR ONE BALL OF YARN IN ONE RING.

TO "DE-KINK" WOOL YARNS

1. Take yarn to your yarn shop if they have a steam press, or your dry cleaner, and have them "steam", not press, the yarn until damp, shake it hard or slap against a table to get the kinks out. Repeat this as many times as necessary to remove kinks. Dry the yarn.

This takes only a few minutes on a steam press and is the best, most convenient and practical way. This will also leave the yarn in better condition than the following methods.

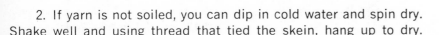

2. If yarn is not soiled, you can dip in cold water and spin dry. Shake well and using thread that tied the skein, hang up to dry.

Sometimes a weight is added to the bottom of the skein to help straighten out the yarn. However, watch the weight is not too heavy for it will stretch the yarn or make creases at the bottom of the skein. Allow for overnight drying.

If yarn is not as fluffy as new yarn, use this in ribbing or place where variance will not be noticed.

3. If yarn is soiled, prepare in hanks as above, wash in cold water with cold water soap. Hang to dry.

4. For small quantities of yarn, some knitters hold yarn over steam from tea kettle and then allow to dry overnight. Take care you do not burn yourself. This is the least successful method, especially if the kinks are well set.

TO "DE-KINK" NYLON AND WOOL

1. Sometimes, if this mixture of yarn has not been knitted too tightly or for too long a time, the kinks can be removed easily by winding into a firm ball or wrapping around a paper tube and allowing to set overnight.

This, however, would not be advisable for fluffy or bulky 50/50 materials. Handle these like wool.

TO "DE-KINK" SYNTHETICS, LINENS, COTTONS

1. If just rewinding these into a ball is not satisfactory, handle the same as wool.

2. If it is undesirable to wash the yarn, some yarn can be wound into ball after passing it through a damp cloth, pulling slightly to remove kinks.

SOME BASIC PATTERN STITCHES

Do memorize your pattern stitches as quickly as possible. You will enjoy the knitting more, catch errors much quicker and save time and energy correcting mistakes.

SEED STITCH 182

(Also called Moss, Corn, Pebble, Rice Stitch)
(Built on K 1, P 1 ribbing)

SEED STITCH

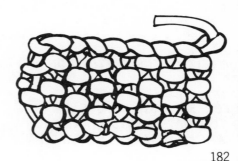

(Worked on an even number of stitches, like 24)
Row 1: *K 1, P 1, repeat between *'s across row.
Row 2: *P 1, K 1 repeat between *'s across row.
Repeat these two rows for pattern.

182

To set up pattern, the first row is *K 1, P 1* across row. The second and succeeding rows, you will begin the rows with the opposite kind of stitch that shows, making knits over purls and purls over knits. If the first stitch that shows is a knit, you will then *P 1, K 1* across the balance of the row. If the first stitch is a purl, you will *K 1, P 1* across the balance of the row.

Seed stitch will look the same on both sides of knitting when finished.

PRACTICE: WORK 6 ROWS OF THE ABOVE PATTERN ON AN EVEN NUMBER OF STITCHES.

SEED STITCH

(Worked on an uneven number of stitches, like 23)

Row 1: *K 1, P 1 repeat between *'s across row, ending K 1.
Repeat this row for pattern.

PRACTICE: WORK 6 ROWS OF SEED STITCH PATTERN ON AN UNEVEN NUMBER OF STITCHES.

MOST PATTERNS CALLING FOR SEED STITCH USE AN UNEVEN NUMBER OF STITCHES SO YOU MAY ALWAYS START EACH ROW WITH A KNIT, WHICH AUTOMATICALLY MAKES THE PATTERN STITCH.

DOUBLE SEED STITCH 183

Double seed stitch (built on K 1, P 1 ribbing, a four row pattern) means that the rows of Seed stitch are built TWO rows high.

An "easy way" to write and work Double Seed stitch ON AN EVEN OR UNEVEN NUMBER OF STITCHES, is:

Row 1: *K 1, P 1, repeat between *'s across row.
Row 2: Work in established ribbing pattern across row.
Row 3: *P 1, K 1, repeat between *'s across row.
Row 4: Work in established ribbing pattern across row.
Repeat these four rows for pattern.

In other words, the first row sets up the pattern which you keep until two rows have been worked. Then you alternate the kind of stitch that shows and this row is built for two rows. The whole pattern is then repeated.

Most instructions for the Double Seed stitch pattern are written as follows:

DOUBLE SEED STITCH

(Worked on an even number of stitches, like 24)
Rows 1 and 4: *K 1, P 1, repeat between *'s across row.
Rows 2 and 3: *P 1, K 1, repeat between *'s across row.
Repeat these four rows for pattern.

183

You will note that Rows 1 and 4, then 2 and 3 have the same directions and therefore, are written only one time.

DOUBLE SEED STITCH 184
(Built on K 2, P 2, making a block pattern)

(Multiple of 4)
Rows 1 and 2: *K 2, P 2, repeat between *'s across row.
Rows 3 and 4: *P 2, K 2, repeat between *'s across row.

184

USE END OF YARN AS GUIDE FOR KEEPING RECORD OF ROWS.

When the knitted piece has the same pattern on both sides, use tail end of beginning yarn as a clue as to whether you are on the even or the uneven numbered row, the right or wrong side of knitting, or when ribbing pattern will change.

When working Row 1 of Double Seed stitch, if tail end is to the right, on the next row, of course, it will be to the left. When you alternate the ribbing pattern, notice which side of knitting the yarn end is on. If it is on the right, each time the yarn end appears on the right, you will alternate pattern. If on the left, change. Once you establish this, all chance of errors in rows is eliminated. This principle will be very helpful on a number of pattern stitches.

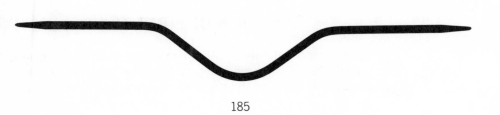

185

CABLE STITCH

A CABLE STITCH, OR TWIST, IS MADE BY TWISTING TWO OR MORE STITCHES. A TWIST IS MADE ON THE KNIT SECTION OF A RIBBING PATTERN, USUALLY WITH PURL STITCHES ON EACH SIDE TO ACCENT THE CABLE SECTION.

HOW TO MAKE A CABLE TWIST

FOR A BASIC CABLE TWIST THE FIRST HALF OF THE STITCHES TO BE TWISTED ARE PUT ON AN EXTRA NEEDLE (CABLE HOLDER OR DOUBLE-POINTED NEEDLE) AND DROPPED TO THE BACK OR THE FRONT OF THE WORK OUT OF THE WAY. THE SECOND HALF OF THE STITCHES ARE KNITTED, THEN THE FIRST HALF OF THE STITCHES ARE KNITTED OFF THE EXTRA NEEDLE.

RIGHT CABLE   *LEFT CABLE*

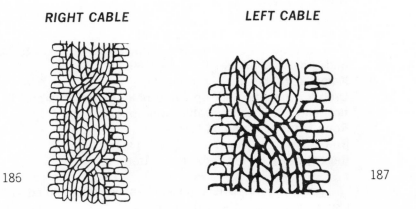

186   187

IF THE FIRST HALF OF THE STITCHES ARE DROPPED TO THE BACK OF WORK, CABLE WILL SPIRAL TO RIGHT. IF DROPPED TO FRONT OF WORK, CABLE WILL SPIRAL TO LEFT. 185 187

THE CABLE HOLDER OR DOUBLE POINTED NEEDLE WILL HAVE A POINT AT EACH END, ONE END TO SLIP THE STITCHES ON AND THE OTHER END TO KNIT THE STITCHES OFF.

LET'S WORK A CABLE TWIST ON 4 KNIT STITCHES AS FOLLOWS:

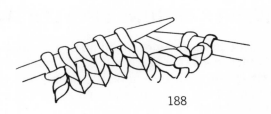

188

SLIP (PURLWISE) 2 KNIT STITCHES TO CABLE HOLDER AND DROP THESE TO BACK OF WORK. 189

K 2 STITCHES FROM LEFT NEEDLE. DROP LEFT NEEDLE.

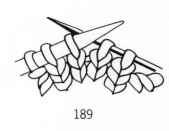

189

PICK UP CABLE HOLDER WITH LEFT HAND (BEING SURE THAT STITCHES ARE FLAT AND HAVE NOT BEEN TWISTED) AND K 2 STITCHES FROM CABLE HOLDER. 190

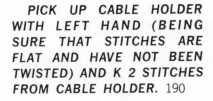

190

CABLE TWIST HAS BEEN MADE. 191

191

NUMBER OF ROWS BETWEEN TWISTS

Cables will have an uneven number of rows between twists. On basic cables, a 4-stitch cable will have a minimum of 5 rows between twists (a 6-row pattern); a 6 stitch cable will have 7 rows between twists (an 8-row pattern); and an 8 stitch cable a minimum of 9 rows between twists (a 10-row pattern).

Many times patterns will vary and use a different number of rows between cables, as a twist on the 6th, 12th, and 24th rows, making a 24-row pattern. Variations are unlimited.

COUNTING ROWS BETWEEN TWISTS

It is difficult to count the number of rows between cable twists, so I recommend always using a row counter. This will save time, assure correct knitting and eliminate possible disappointment later. If you get two few or two many rows between twists, it may not be obvious until piece is finished. You will probably say, " I don't think it shows that much and besides, I don't want to do it over." Don't kid yourself! It does show! It is up to you whether you redo it or not but you CAN do it right. After learning the hard way, next time be SURE with a row counter.

POSITION OF FIRST TWIST

There is no set rule in which row first twist must begin. The basic cable begins first twist on the fifth row. However, some of our newer patterns twist on the third and even on the first row.

PLACING OF CABLE

You may use as many or as few cables across rows as you desire. The combinations are unlimited. Cables can be used as trim and very pretty garments can be made using cabling in place of ribbing edges of sweaters and in strips to be sewed to edges of knits like piping.

BASIC WAYS TO WRITE CABLE STITCH PATTERN
(FOR ROPE CABLE TO RIGHT)

EXAMPLE 1

This manner of writing is used most today to avoid any confusion and misunderstanding of instructions. Each row is written out and the series of 8 rows are repeated over and over to make pattern, as:

CABLE PATTERN (6 sts) 188

Row 1: P 1, K 4, P 1.
Row 2: K 1, P 4, K 1.
Row 3 and 4: Same as Rows 1 and 2.
Row 5: (Cable twist row) P 1, slip next 2 stitches to cable holder and DROP TO BACK OF WORK. 189
K next 2 stitches from left needle.
Drop left needle, pick up cable holder (being careful to keep work flat) and K 2 stitches (cable twist made), P 1.
Rows 6 and 8: Same as Row 2.
Row 7: Same as Row 1.
Repeat these 8 rows for cable pattern.

After several twists have been worked, cabled ribs will look like a rope — spirals to the right.

EXAMPLE 2

CABLE PATTERN (6 sts)
Row 1: P 1, K 4, P 1.
Row 2: K 1, P 4, K 1.
Rows 3 and 4: Same as 1 and 2.
Row 5: (Cable twist row) P 1, slip next 2 stitches to cable holder and drop to back of work, K next 2 sts from left needle. Drop left needle, pick up cable holder (being careful to keep work flat) and K 2 stitches (cable twist made), P 1.
Continue in pattern as established, MAKING CABLE TWISTS EVERY 8TH ROW.

This manner of writing instructions is seldom used today but sometimes needs a little explanation for beginners who ask questions like these:

"Do I have only 3 rows before next twist?"
"Do you work 8 rows, then cable again?"
"Do I work cable on 8th row from beginning?"
"Do I have 7 rows between cable twists?"

Seven rows between cable twists is the correct answer here. After cable twist is made, you work Rows 6-7-8-1-2-3-4.

To eliminate any further confusion with this Example 2, when I reach the cable twist row, I immediately re-number this row, calling it by the LARGEST NUMBER OF ROWS IN PATTERN.

If this is an 8-row pattern, and cable begins on Row 5, I re-number the twist row, Row 8. Then I work 7 rows of pattern and twist on the right side of work, Row 8.

If pattern contains 12 rows, the cable twist row would be numbered Row 12, working 11 rows between twists.

Re-numbering the rows like this will mean that the right side of the knitting will be even numbered rows and the wrong side uneven numbered rows.

The cable pattern learned here is called a Rope cable. Others frequently used are called Horseshoe or Calla Lily Cable, Plaited or Braided Cable, Hongkong Cable and a Right Twist and Left Twist which are built on two stitches only.

BASIC TWIST STITCH
(Two stitch cable)

192

(RIGHT TWIST) 193
PATTERN (Multiple of 2)
Skip the first stitch on left needle. 194
Knit the second stitch but do not pull off stitches. 195
K the first stitch skipped. 196, 197
Pull off both stitches. 192

193

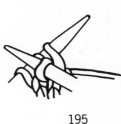

194

195

196

197

To practice Right Twist, work following pattern:
(Multiple of 4 + 2)
Cast on 10 sts.
Row 1: *Make a Right Twist, P 2, repeat between *'s across row ending with a Right Twist.
Row 2: *P 2, K 2, repeat between *'s across row, ending with P 2.
Row 3: *K 2, P 2, repeat between *'s across row, ending with K 2.
Row 4: Same as Row 2.
Repeat these four rows for pattern.

(LEFT TWIST) 199

PATTERN (Multiple of 2)
With right needle and AT BACK OF WORK, skip the first stitch on left needle.
Knit in the BACK of the second stitch but do not pull off stitches. 200, 201
K the first stitch skipped. 202
203 Pull off both stitches. 198

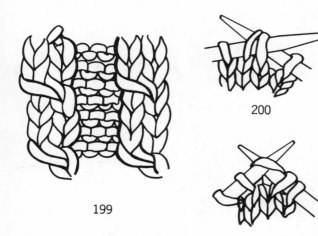

198

199

200

201

202

203

To practice Left Twist, work following pattern:
(Multiple of 4 + 2)
Cast on 10 sts.
Row 1: *Make a Left Twist, P 2, repeat between *'s across row ending with a Left Twist.
Row 2: *P 2, K 2, repeat between *'s across row, ending with P 2.
Row 3: *K 2, P 2, repeat between *'s across row, ending K 2.
Row 4: Same as Row 2.
Repeat these four rows for pattern.

FABRIC STITCH 204

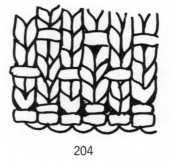

204

PATTERN (Multiple of 2 plus 1)
Row 1: *K 1, yarn forward, sl 1, yarn back, repeat between *'s across row.
Rows 2 and 4: Purl.
Row 3: K 2, *yarn forward, sl 1, yarn back, K 1, repeat between *'s across row ending K 2.
Repeat these four rows for pattern.

VARIATION OF THE FABRIC STITCH 205

This is an excellent substitute for ribbing and borders. It is very easy to do and uses same size needle as used on body of sweater.

205

PATTERN (Uneven number of stitches)
Row 1: K.
ROW 2: K 1, *with yarn at back, slip 1 stitch as if to purl, K 1, repeat between *'s to end.
Row 3: K.
Row 4: K 2, *with yarn at back, slip 1 st, K 1, repeat between *'s across row, ending K 2.
Repeat these 4 rows for pattern.

QUAKER RIB 206

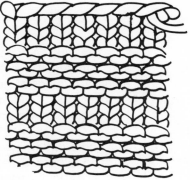

PATTERN (Any number of stitches)
Row 1: K 1 row.
Row 2: P 1 row.
Rows 3 and 4: K 1 row.
Row 5: P 1 row.
Row 6: K 1 row.
or
PATTERN (Any number of stitches)
*K 1 row, P 1 row, K 1 row, repeat between *'s for pattern stitch.

206

BASIC POPCORN STITCH 207

PATTERN (Multiple of 4 plus 2)
Row 1: P.
Row 2: K 1 *(K 1, P 1, K 1) in next stitch (3 stitches now made in one stitch), P 3 tog.
Repeat between *'s across row ending K 1.
Row 3: P.
Row 4: K 1, *P 3 tog., (K 1, P 1, K 1) in next stitch, repeat between *'s across row ending with K 1.
Repeat these 4 rows for pattern.

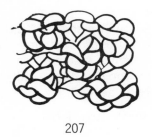

207

208

POPCORN STITCH ON STOCKINETTE 208

PATTERN (Multiple of 4 + 3)
Row 1: K.
Row 2: P.

Row 3: K 1, *(K in front and back of stitch 5 times). With left needle, lift first stitch made of popcorn over the four knits, the second made over the three knits, third made over the two knits, fourth made over the knit (one loop on needle), K 3, repeat between *'s across ending K 1.
Rows 4 and 6: Purl.
Row 5: Knit.
Row 7: K 3, repeat between *'s of Row 3 ending with K 3.
Row 8: Purl.
Repeat these 8 rows for pattern.

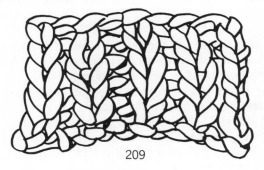

209

FISHERMAN'S RIB 209
(Knit in the row below)

PATTERN (Even number of stitches built on K 1, P 1 ribbing)
Row 1: *K 1, P 1, repeat between *'s across row.
Row 2: K 1, P 1, *K 1 in row below, P 1, repeat between *'s across row. 210, 211
Repeat Row 2 for pattern.

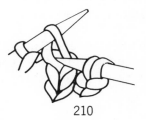

210

211

PATTERN (Even number of stitches, knitting every stitch)
Row 1: K.
Row 2: *K 1, K in row below, repeat between *'s ending K 2.
Repeat Row 2 for pattern.

SOME CHARACTERISTICS OF PATTERN STITCHES

Here are a few of the characteristics of stitches that enter into designing garments and answers in part some of the questions of why certain stitches are used in specific places.

It is interesting to note that a sweater worn with the purl side out (reverse stockinette) will be wider than one with an equal number of stitches if worn with the knit side out. The structure of the Reverse Stockinette stitch tends to spread sideways and will curve to fit the contures of the body, whereas, the knit stitch would have a tendency to lengthen.

In Ribbing, an equal number of rows of Ribbing will be longer than an equal number of rows of Stockinette. At the same time Ribbing pattern lengthens, it will also become more narrow. This will answer your future question as to why ribbed front borders on sweaters are knitted as a separate strip above the waistband. This ribbed border should be 1-½" to 2-½" shorter than the corresponding length of body sweater. This border will keep edges firm, flat and square the corner at bottom of sweater. Any fullness in body of sweater will block in.

The Fabric Stitch will not only resist spreading in width but also in length. This is an important factor in making coats and suits to hold their shape and for using yarns of linen, cotton, etc.

The Seed stitch and Garter stitch are good border patterns for they have the same pattern on both sides and will lay flat. The Garter stitch will pull up some and spread wide. Seed Stitch has a tendency to spread both ways and usually requires smaller needles for border edges or piece worked separately and sewed on.

Lacey patterns, like Mock Cable and Feather and Fan are going to spread more than solid stitches. Consequently, for the same size piece, fewer stitches would be used on a lace pattern than one designed for solid knitting.

Do have some fun experimenting with some of the stitches. Don't be afraid of making mistakes. Make a new stitch! Some of our most interesting pattern stitches have been discovered through errors.

KNITTING PATTERNS

You will do much better knitting on your first sweater if you knit and finish a small item first. On the following pages I have made a number of original patterns for beginning knitters. The TV slippers, Ski Headband, Mittens and Hats are the only patterns that require sewing any seams.

Some patterns have been written with a little more detail than you can expect in pattern books but are as brief as possible. They vary in difficulty from the very easiest to the more interesting lace design.

YOU SHOULD BE ABLE TO DO ALL OF THESE PATTERNS AFTER WORKING STRAIGHT THROUGH THIS MANUAL.

Please note that some of the patterns require a different size needle than No. 8. Also double strands of yarn are used in some patterns. It is not advisable to change the designated yarns, weights of yarns, size of needles, etc., unless helped by an expert knitter or an instructress.

BLOCKING

For items made from this book, block the knitting as follows:
1. Have blocked by a professional if service is available.
2. Have a dry cleaner steam into shape.
3. Or, if doing the blocking yourself, pin piece right side down on ironing board or flat surface that will allow steaming and pinning. Cover with damp cloth and press lightly. A steam iron is excellent here. DO NOT let the weight of the iron rest on the knitting. Let dry thoroughly. Sew and steam seams if needed.

HAPPY KNITTING!

NOTES

GARTER STITCH SCARF
10" x 42"

2 — 4 oz. skeins Knitting Worsted
1 — pair No. 8 knitting needles
1 — No. 5 aluminum crochet hook
GAUGE: 4-½ sts = 1"

SCARF
With No. 8 needles, cast on 50 sts.
Knit every row until piece measures 42" or desired length.
Bind off.
Weave in ends.
Block.
FRINGE:
Make fringe on a 3" card, placing two 6" strands in every other stitch on each end of scarf.

STOCKINETTE STITCH SCARF
WITH GARTER STITCH BORDERS
10" x 42"

2 — 4 oz. skeins Knitting Worsted
1 — pair No. 8 knitting needles
GAUGE: 5 sts = 1"

SCARF:
With No. 8 needles, cast on 48 sts.
Work in Garter stitch until measures 1".
Row 1: K 5, P 38, K 5.
Row 2: K.
Repeat these two rows until piece measures 41" or desired length from beginning.
Work in Garter stitch for 1".
Bind off.
Weave in ends.
Block.

BROKEN RIB SCARF
9" x 42"

2 — 4 oz. skeins Knitting Worsted
1 — pair No. 10 knitting needles
GAUGE: 5 sts = 1"

BROKEN RIB PATTERN (Multiple of 4 plus 3)
SCARF:
With No. 10 needles, cast on 43 sts.
Row 1: *K 2, P 2, repeat between *'s across row ending K 2, P 1.
Repeat this row for pattern.
(NOTICE THE FIRST KNIT STITCH OF THE K 2 FALLS ON THE KNIT STITCH RIB OF EACH ROW.)
Work in pattern until piece measures 42" or desired length.
Bind off in ribbing pattern.
Weave in ends.
Block.
FRINGE:
Make fringe over 5" card. Tie in two 10" strands every other stitch on each end of scarf.

CABLE STITCH SCARF
WITH GARTER STITCH BORDER
10" x 42"

2 — 4 oz. skeins Knitting Worsted
1 — pair No. 8 knitting needles
GAUGE: 5 sts = 1"

CABLE PATTERN STITCH (Multiple of 7 plus 3)
Row 1: P 1, K 1, P 1, *K 4, P 1, K 1, P 1, repeat between *'s across row.
Row 2: K 3, *P 4, K 3 repeat between *'s across row.
Row 3: Same as Row 1.
Row 4: Same as Row 2.
Row 5: P 1, K 1, P 1, *slip 2 sts to cable holder, drop to BACK of work, K 2, K 2 from cable holder, P 1, K 1, P 1, repeat between *'s across row.
Row 6: Same as Row 2.
Row 7: Same as Row 1.
Row 8: Same as Row 2.
Repeat these 8 rows for pattern.

SCARF:
With No. 8 needles, cast on 48 sts.
Work in Garter stitch for 1".
Row 1: K 5 sts, work Row 1 of pattern, K 5 sts.
Row 2: K 5 sts, work Row 2 of pattern, K 5 sts.
Continue in this manner, keeping 5 sts on each border edge in Garter stitch and repeating 8 rows of pattern in the center of scarf.
Work until piece measures 41" or length desired, ending with Row 1.
Work in Garter stitch for 1".
Bind off.
Block.

POPCORN STITCH SCARF
WITH GARTER STITCH BORDERS
10" x 42"

double for shawl

30 x 80
82

2 — 4 oz. skeins Knitting Worsted
1 — pair No. 10 knitting needles
GAUGE: 5 sts = 1"

POPCORN PATTERN STITCH (Multiple of 4 plus 2)
Row 1: P.
Row 2: K 1, *(K 1, P 1, K 1) in next st. (3 stitches made in one stitch), P 3 tog., repeat between *'s across row ending K 1.
Row 3: P.
Row 4: K 1, *P 3 tog., (K 1, P 1, K 1) in next st., repeat between *'s across row ending with K 1.
Repeat these 4 rows for pattern.

SCARF:
With No. 10 needles cast on 48 sts.
Work in Garter stitch for 1".
Row 1: K 5, work Row 1 of pattern, K 5.
Row 2: K 5, work Row 2 of pattern, K 5.
Row 3: K 5, work Row 3 of pattern, K 5.
Row 4. K 5, work Row 4 of pattern, K 5.
Continuing 5 sts on each side in Garter stitch and repeating 4 pattern rows in center section, work even until 41" or desired length.
Work in Garter stitch for 1".
Bind off.
Block.

FANCY PATTERNED SCARF
WITH GARTER STITCH BORDERS
10" x 42"

2 — 4 oz. skeins Knitting Worsted
1 — pair No. 8 knitting needles
GAUGE: 5 sts = 1"

PATTERN STITCH: (32 sts.)
NOTE: WHEN SLIPPING STITCHES FOR DECREASING, SLIP KNIT-WISE SO LOOP WILL BE FLAT.
Row 1: K.
Row 2: K 4, P 8, K 8, P 8, K 4.
Row 3: K 1, P 2, *K 2 tog., K 3, pick up next bar between sts and place on left-hand needle, K 1 st on back of this loop and another st on front of loop (2 sts. increased), K 3, S1 1, K 1, PSSO, P 6; repeat between *'s once ending P 2, K 1 instead of P 6.
Row 4: K 3, P 10, K 6, P 10, K 3.
Row 5: K 1, P 1, *K 2 tog., K 3, pick up next bar between sts and K 1 st on back of this loop (1st increased), K 2, pick up next bar between sts and K 1 st on back of this loop, K 3, S1 1, K 1, PSSO*, P 4; repeat between *'s once ending P 1, K 1 instead of P 4.
Row 6: K 2, P 12, K 4, P 12, K 2.
Row 7: K 1, *K 2 tog., K 3, pick up next bar between sts and K 1 st on back of this loop, K 4, pick up next bar between sts and K 1 st on back of this loop, K 3, S1 1, K 1, PSSO *, P 2; repeat between *'s once, ending K 1 instead of P 2.
Row 8: K 1, P 14, K 2, P 14, K 1.
Row 9: *K 2 tog., K 3, pick up next bar between sts and K 1 st on back of this loop, K 6, pick up next bar between sts and K 1 st on back of this loop, K 3, S1 1, K 1, PSSO; repeat from* once.
Row 10: K 1, P 30, K 1.
Repeat these 10 rows for pattern.

SCARF:
With No. 8 needles, cast on 48 sts. Work in Garter stitch for 1-½".
Row 1: K 8, work Row 1 of pattern, K 8.
Row 2: K 8, work Row 2 of pattern, K 8.
Continue in this manner keeping 8 stitches on each side in border pattern and repeat 10 row pattern in center section until piece measures approximately 40" ending with Row 10.
Work Garter stitch for 1-½".
Bind off.
Block.
Trim with fringe if desired.

HOW TO DESIGN YOUR OWN SCARF 212
10" x 42"

2 — 4 oz. skeins Knitting Worsted
1 — pair No. 8 knitting needles
GAUGE: 5 sts = 1"

BORDER:
Let's use a 1" border — 5 sts on each side. (Markers can be placed to separate the border edges from the center section if desired.)
PATTERNED CENTER SECTION:
Since the number of stitches varies with the kind of pattern stitch you will make, use the closest number sufficient for an 8" center section, approximately 40 sts.
NUMBER OF STITCHES TO BE USED:
Using the basic Popcorn stitch pattern as written on Page 61, the center pattern section in this stitch would need a multiple of 4 plus 2. Multiply 4 x 9 = 36 sts, plus 2, totaling 38 sts. Therefore, since 38 is the closest to the needed 40 sts, center section will have 38 sts, borders 5 sts on each side, making a total of 48 sts.
SCARF:
With No. 8 needles, cast on 48 sts.
Work in Garter Stitch for 1".
Row 1: K 5, work Row 1 of pattern, K 5.
Row 2: K 5, work Row 2 of pattern, K 5.
Continue working in this manner, keeping borders in Garter stitch and repeating the four pattern rows in center section until piece measures 41" or desired length.
Work in Garter stitch for 1". Bind off. Weave in ends. Block.

A scarf or muffler makes a lovely personal gift. It is very usable and is an excellent way to use up left-over yarn.

Variations of colors and pattern stitches are unlimited.

Borders can be done in different stitches and colors. Trimmings and appliques can be sewed on.

Initials can be worked in embroidery or duplicate stitch.

Have some fun and create your own scarf design using YOUR favorite stitches.

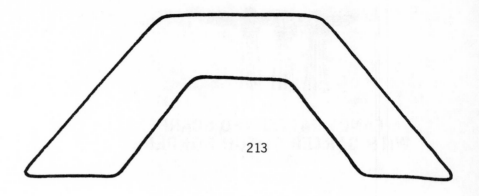

213

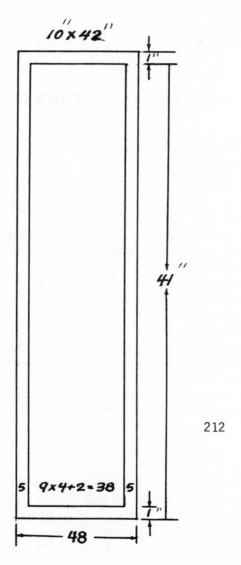

212

MAN'S CONTOUR NECK SCARF 213

1 — 4 oz. skein Knitting Worsted
1 — pair No. 11 knitting needles
NOTE: ENTIRE SCARF IS KNITTED IN GARTER STITCH WITH DOUBLE YARN. (DIVIDE SKEIN AND ROLL INTO TWO BALLS. TAKE ONE END OF YARN FROM EACH BALL, HOLD TOGETHER AND KNIT AS ONE PIECE OF YARN.)

SCARF:
Using two strands of yarn and No. 11 needles, cast on 18 sts.
FIRST DIAGONAL SECTION:
Row 1: K 1, inc. 1 st in next st (Method No. 1), K across row (19 sts).
ROW 2: K 1, K 2 tog., K across row (18 sts).
Repeat these two rows until piece measuring up through center of piece is approximately 13″, ending with Row 1 (19 sts).
NECK SECTION:
Work even on 19 sts for 8″, measuring straight edge of neck, ending with First Diagonal Section laying to your right. Turn.
SECOND DIAGONAL SECTION: (Will lay in same direction as First Diagonal Section)
Row 1: K 1, K 2 tog., K across row (18 sts).
Row 2: K 1, inc. 1st in next st, K across row (19 sts).
Repeat these two rows, until piece measures same as First Diagonal Section, ending with Row 1 (18 sts).
Bind off. Block.

BABY BLANKET IN STOCKINETTE STITCH
WITH GARTER STITCH BORDER
25" x 30"

3 — 4 oz. skeins Knitting Worsted
1 — pair No. 8 knitting needles
GAUGE: 5 sts = 1"
BLANKET:
With No. 8 needles cast 120 sts.
Work in Garter stitch for 2-½" (measuring up to the needle).
Row 1: (wrong side) K 13 (for border), P 94, K 13 (for border).
Row 2: K.
Repeat these two rows until piece measures approximately 27-½" ending with Row 1.
Work for 2-½" in Garter stitch.
Bind off. Weave in ends. Block.
If desired, blanket can be trimmed with cross stitch, duplicate stitch, embroidery or appliques.

BABY BLANKET IN STRIPS OF RIBBING AND STOCKINETTE WITH GARTER STITCH BORDERS
27" x 30"

3 — 4 oz. skeins Knitting Worsted
1 — pair No. 8 kniting needles
GAUGE: 4-½ sts = 1"

BLANKET:
With No. 8 needles cast on 124 sts.
Work in Garter stitch for 1".
Rows 1 and 3: K 5 sts for border, *K 2, P 2, repeat between *'s across to last 7 sts, K 2, K 5 sts for border.
Rows 2 and 4: K 5 sts for border, *P 2, K 2, repeat between *'s across to last 7 sts, P 2, K 5 sts for border.
Rows 5 and 7: K.
Rows 6 and 8: K 5 sts for border, P across to last 5 sts, K 5 sts for border.
Repeat these 8 rows until piece measures approximately 29 ", ending with Row 4.
Work in Garter stitch for 1".
Bind off. Weave in ends. Block.

BABY BLANKET IN BLOCK PATTERN
WITH GARTER STITCH BORDER
29" x 32"

3 — 4 oz. skeins Knitting Worsted
1 — pair No. 9 needles
GAUGE: 4-½ sts = 1"

BLOCK PATTERN (Multiple of 8)
BLANKET:
With No. 9 needles cast on 130 sts.
Work in Garter Stitch for 2-½".
Row 1: (right side) K 13, *K 2, P 2, repeat between *'s on 104 sts, K 13.
Row 2: K 13, work ribbing across 104 sts (this is K 2, P 2), K 13.
Row 3: K.
Row 4: K 13, P 104, K 13.
Row 5: K 13, *P 2, K 2, repeat between *'s on 104 sts, K 13.
Row 6: K 13, work ribbing across 104 sts (this is P 2, K 2), K 13.
Row 7: K.
Row 8: K 13, P 104, K 13.
Repeat these 8 rows until piece measures approximately 29 -½" ending with Row 2 or Row 6.
Work in Garter stitch for 2-½".
Bind off. Weave in ends. Block.

BABY BLANKET WITH CENTER BLOCK AND BORDERS IN SEED STITCH
29″ x 36″

3 — 4 oz. skeins Knitting Worsted
1 — pair No. 8 knitting needles
GAUGE: 4-½ sts = 1″

BLANKET:
With No. 8 needles, cast on 131 sts.
SEED STITCH BORDER:
*K 1, P 1 repeat between *'s across row ending K 1.
Repeat this row until 3-½″ from beg.
STOCKINETTE SECTION:
Row 1: Work 17 sts in Seed st, K 97 sts, work 17 sts in Seed st.
Row 2: Work 17 sts in Seed st, P 97, work 17 sts in Seed st.
Repeat these 2 rows until 8-½″ from beg.
CENTER SECTION:
Row 1: Work 17 sts in Seed st, K 25, work 47 sts in Seed stitch, K 25, work 17 sts in Seed stitch.
Row 2: Work 17 sts in Seed stitch, P 25, work 47 sts in Seed st, P 25, work 17 sts in Seed st.
Repeat these two rows until piece measures 27-½″ from beg.
STOCKINETTE SECTION:
Repeat the two rows from above Stockinette Section until piece measures 32-½″ from beg.
SEED STITCH BORDER:
Work as above for 3-½″.
Bind off in pattern. Weave in ends. Block.

DOUBLE CABLE BABY BLANKET WITH GARTER STITCH BORDERS
26″ x 28″

3 — 4 oz. skeins Knitting Worsted
1 — pair No. 10 knitting needles
1 — cable holder
GAUGE: 4-½ sts = 1″

PATTERN STITCH (Multiple of 15 plus 1)
Row 1: (right side) K 1, *P 3, K 8, P 3, K 1, repeat from * across row.
Row 2: K 4, *P 8, K 7, repeat from * across row ending P 8, K 4.
Row 3: Same as Row 1.
Row 4: Same as Row 2.
Row 5: K 1, *P 3, s1 next 2 sts onto cable holder, drop to BACK of work, K 2, K 2 from cable holder, s1 next 2 sts to cable holder, drop to FRONT of work, K 2, K 2 from holder, P 3, K 1, repeat from * across row.
Row 6: Same as Row 2.
Row 7: Same as Row 1.
Row 8: Same as Row 2.
Row 9: Same as Row 1.
Row 10: Same as Row 2.
Repeat these 10 rows for pattern.

BLANKET:
With No. 10 needles cast on 116 sts.
Work in Garter stitch for 1″.
Row 1: K 5 sts, work Row 1 of pattern, K 5 sts.
Row 2: K 5 sts, work Row 2 of pattern, K 5 sts.
Continue in this manner, knitting 5 sts at each end of each row and working 10 row pattern in center of blanket until blanket measures approximately 27″, ending with Row 9 of pattern.
Work in Garter stitch for 1″.
Bind off. Weave in ends. Block.

MOCK CABLE BABY BLANKET
WITH FRINGE TRIM
27" x 27"

3 — 4 oz. skeins Knitting Worsted
1 — pair No. 8 knitting needles
GAUGE: 3 patterns equal 2"

KNIT TIP: ROWS 2 and 3 WILL HAVE MORE STITCHES THAN ROWS 1 AND 4.

BLANKET:
With No. 8 needles, cast on 130 sts.
Row 1: (wrong side) *K 1, P 2, repeat between *'s, ending K 1.
Row 2: *P 1, K 1, YO, K 1, repeat between *'s ending P 1.
Row 3: *K 1, P 3, repeat between *'s ending K 1.
Row 4: *P 1, yarn to back of work, s1 1 purlwise, K 2 sts, PSSO (pass the slip stitch over the TWO knit stitches), repeat between *'s across row, ending P 1.
Repeat these 4 rows until piece measures 27", ending with Row 1. Bind off in ribbing pattern. Weave in ends. Block.

Fringe: Make fringe on card 3-½" in depth. Tie one 7" strand in every other stitch on all four sides of blanket. Trim ends.

BABY BLANKET OR CARRIAGE ROBE IN FEATHER
AND FAN PATTERN WITH GARTER BORDERS
21" x 24"

2 — 4 oz. skeins Knitting Worsted
1 — pair No. 8 knitting needles
GAUGE: 5-½ sts = 1"
PATTERN (Multiple of 18 sts)
BLANKET:
With No. 8 needles, cast on 116 sts.
K 6 rows in Garter stitch.
Row 1: K.
Row 2: K4, P to last 4 sts, K4.
Row 3: K4, (K2 tog) 3 times, *(YO, K1) 6 times, (K2 tog) 6 times, repeat from * across row 4 times MORE, ending row with (YO, K1) 6 times, (K2 tog) 3 times, K4 (116 sts.)
Row 4: K.
Repeat these 4 rows for pattern.
Work even until piece measures approximately 23", ending with Row 4.
K 5 rows in Garter stitch. Bind off. Block.

DEEP TOBOGGAN

2 — 40 gram balls Mohair
1 — 2 oz. or 4 oz. skein Knitting Worsted
1 — pair No. 11 knitting needles
1 cable holder

NOTE: DOUBLE YARN, ONE STRAND MOHAIR AND ONE STRAND KNITTING WORSTED (HELD TOGETHER), IS USED THROUGHOUT THIS HAT.

TOBOGGAN:
With No. 11 needles, cast on 48 sts.
K 1, P 1 in ribbing until 11" from beginning or desired length.

SHAPE TOP:
*S1 K stitch on left needle to right needle, s1 P st on left needle to cable holder and hold at back of work, s1 K st on right needle back to left needle and K 2 tog. S1 P on cable holder to left needle and P 2 tog. Repeat between *'s across row. (24 sts)
K 1, P 1 in ribbing for 5 more rows.
(Right side) K 2 tog across row. (12 sts)
Break yarn leaving 18" for sewing.

FINISHING:
Using large yarn sewing needle, pull end through stitches on needle and draw up stitches tightly; on wrong side (ridge of purl stitches), overcast side seams tog. Weave in ends. Block if necessary.

TRIMMING:
Make large Pom Pon of mohair only and tie on, or make an 8", large tassel and tie on.
For men for hunting or skiing, make small pom pon and turn back edges twice.

CABLE EARWARMER

1 — 2 oz. skein Knitting Worsted
1 — pair No. 8 knitting needles
1 — cable holder

1 — row counter
1 — package stitch markers
1 — yarn sewing needle

TIE:
With No. 8 needles cast on 4 sts.
*K 1, P 1, repeat between *'s across row. Work until tie is 14" long.

EAR LUG:
Working in Garter Stitch, *Inc. 1 st in first st (Method No. 1), K across row.
Repeat between *'s until 22 sts are on needle.

HEADBAND CABLE SECTION:
Using row counter, work as follows:
Row 1: K 4, place marker on right needle, K 3, P 1, K 6, P 1, K 3, place marker on right needle, K 4.
Row 2: K 4, slip marker to right needle, P 3, K 1, P 6, K 1, P 3, slip marker to right needle, K 4.
(Markers are slipped each time they are reached and the first 4 and last 4 sts are knitted on every row for border edge.)
Row 3: Same as Row 1 (except markers are already placed).

Row 4: Same as Row 2.
Row 5: (Cable twist row) K 4, s1 marker, K 3, P 1, (make cable twist as follows) slip purlwise first 3 sts to cable holder and drop to FRONT of work, K next 3 sts on left needle, (put down left needle), pick up cable holder, K 3 sts on cable holder (cable twist made), P 1, K 3, slip marker, K 4.
Row 6: Same as Row 2.
Row 7: Same as Row 3.
Row 8: Same as Row 2.
Repeat Rows 1 through 8 until HEADBAND CABLE SECTION measures 10-½" to 11" at a CABLE TWIST ROW. Work an additional 4 rows after last cable twist (this ends with Row 1).

EAR LUG:
Working in Garter Stitch, *K 2 tog, K across row.
Repeat between *'s until 4 sts remain.

TIE:
*K 1, P 1 repeat between *'s until piece measures 14". Bind off. Weave in ends. Block.

70

TV OR BED SLIPPERS
(Medium size)

1 — 4 oz. skein Knitting Worsted
1 — pair No. 8 knitting needles
1 — sewing needle for yarn

GAUGE: 5 sts equals 1″

SLIPPERS: (Make 2)
Using No. 8 needles, cast on 42 sts (using Method No. 3 Knitwise).
Row 1: K across row.
Row 2: K 14, P 14, K 14.
Repeat Rows 1 and 2 until Stockinette section measures 6″.

SHAPING TOP OF SLIPPER:
Bind off 5 sts at beg. of next 2 rows as follows:
Bind off 5 sts; work in established pattern across row. Turn.
Bind off 5 sts; work in established pattern across row.
Keeping in pattern, work until Stockinette section is 7-½″, or desired length, from beginning.

TOE SECTION:
*K 2, P 2, repeat between *'s for 2″.
Cut yarn, leaving 18″ end for sewing.

FINISHING:

TOE: Using sewing needle, drawn yarn through each stitch on needle and drawn up stitches together. Go through these stitches against for reinforcing. Fold slipper lengthwise, with wrong side together, and continue to sew edges together by overcasting stitches along ribbed edges, garter stitch and bound-off sts on front. Fasten off.

HEEL: Beginning at top edge, overcast edges of heel together with yarn to stockinette section. Picking up one thread of each stitch on edge of Stockinette section, pull into a circle and fasten well. Weave in ends. Block. Trim with pom pons, cord, ribbon, tassels, etc.

SKI HEADBAND

1 — 1 oz. Knitting Worsted
1 — pair No. 6 knitting needles
1 — yarn sewing needle
GAUGE: 5 sts = 1″

HEADBAND:
With No. 6 needles, cast on 20 sts (suggest Method No. 3).
Row 1: P 1, K 1, P 1, K 1, P 12 (Center section) K 1, P 1, K 1, P 1.
Row 2: K 1, P 1, K 1, P 1, K 12, P 1, K 1, P 1, K 1.
Repeat these 2 rows for 6″, ending with Row 1.

DECREASING TO NARROW HEAD SECTION:
Rows 1-3-5: Rib 4 sts, K 2 tog. (to lean to left as on Page 47). Work until 6 sts remain, K 2 tog (to lean to right as on Page 47). Rib 4 sts.
Rows 2-4-6: Work across row in established pattern. Work even on 14 sts until piece measures 12-¼″ from beginning, ending on wrong side.

INCREASING TO WIDE HEAD SECTION:
Rows 1-3-5: Rib 4 sts, K 1, inc. 1 st (Method No. 3), work across row until 5 sts remain, inc. 1 st (Method No. 3), K 1, rib 4 sts.
Rows 2-4-6: Work across row in established pattern.

Work even on 20 sts until piece measures 19″ from beginning, or desired length.
Bind off leaving 10″ end to sew back seam.
BLOCK: Pin piece right side down on ironing board. Cover with damp cloth and steam press lightly. Let dry thoroughly.
FINISHING: Using blunt end yarn needle, overcast together the cast-on and bound-off edges, keeping seam flat as possible. Weave in ends.

"BALL" HAT

1 — 2 oz. skein Knitting Worsted and
4 — 10 gram balls 100% angora
1 — pair each No. 6 and No. 11 knitting needles
1 — large yarn sewing needle
1 — cable holder
NOTE: DOUBLE YARN, ONE STRAND EACH OF KNITTING WORSTED AND ANGORA, IS USED THROUGHOUT THIS HAT.

HAT:
With No. 6 needles and double yarn, cast on 60 sts. K 1, P 1 in ribbing for 6 rows.
Change to No. 11 needles and K 1, P 1 in ribbing for 1 row.
FISHERMAN'S RIB SECTION:
Row 1: K 1, P 1, *K 1 in row below, P 1, repeat between *'s across row.
Repeat this row until piece measures 6-½" or desired length.
TOP SHAPING: (right side)
*S1 K stitch on left needle to right needle, slip P stitch on left needle to cable holder and hold at BACK of work, slip k stitch on right needle back to left needle and K 2 tog.
S1 P on cable holder to left needle and P 2 tog.
Repeat between *'s across row.
K 1, P 1 in ribbing for 5 more rows.
(Right side) K 2 tog. across row.
Break yarn leaving 18" to sew.
FINISHING: Using large yarn sewing needle, pull end through stitches on needle and draw up stitches tightly; on wrong side (ridge of purl stitches) overcast side seams together.
Weave in ends. No blocking required on this hat.

MITTENS
(Will fit either hand)

1 — 4 oz. skeins Knitting Worsted
2 — stitch holders

Child's—5 to 8 yrs.	Child's—9 to 12 yrs.	Woman's Medium
1 pair each	1 pair each	1 pair each
No. 2 and No. 4	No. 3 and No. 6	No. 4 and No. 8
knitting needles	knitting needles	knitting needles

NOTE: Where three numbers are given, as 10-10-12, use the first number for small size, second for middle size and third for woman's size. All other numbers are the same for all sizes.

MITTEN: (Make 2).
Starting at cuff edge with small needles, cast on 36 sts.
Work in ribbing of *K 1, P 1* for 2"-2-½"-3".
Changing to large needles, K 1 row, P 1 row, K 1 row, P 1 row.
INCREASE FOR THUMB:
(All increases for thumb will be Method No. 3 knitwise.)
Row 1: K 17, inc. 1 st, K 2 sts, inc. 1 st, K 17.
Row 2: P.
Row 3: K 17, inc. 1 st, K 4 sts, inc. 1 st, K 17.
Row 4: P.
Continue working as above, increasing 2 more stitches on each K row until 12-12-14 sts (including increases) are in the thumb section, ending with the K row (46-46-48 sts).
DIVIDING THUMB SECTION FROM HAND SECTION:
P 17 sts and s1 these stitches to a stitch holder, P 12-12-14 sts for thumb, s1 remaining 17 sts·to a second stitch holder.
THUMB: Work 10-10-12 rows in Stockinette stitch.
Dec. row: K 2 tog. across row.
Break yarn, leaving about 6" for sewing. Using sewing needle, draw end of yarn through each loop on needle, pull off needle, draw stitches together. Leave for sewing later.
JOINING HAND SECTION:
S1 stitches from each holder to separate needles. On purl side attach yarn at beginning of last 17 sts. P 17 sts.
Next row: K across 34 sts. (Hand section joined).
Continue in Stockinette stitch until mitten measures 6-¼"-7"-8" from beginning, ending with a P row.
SHAPING FOR TOP:
Row 1: *K 2, K 2 tog., repeat between *'s across row.
Row 2: P.
Row 3: *K 1, K 2 tog., repeat between *'s across row.
Row 4: P.
Row 5: K 2 tog. across row.
Break yarn, leaving about 12" for sewing.

FINISHING:
Draw yarn through remaining stitches and fasten. Sew seam at side of mitten and side of thumb. Weave bottom of thumb and palm of mitten together. Weave in ends. Block.

HOW TO MAKE FRINGE

1 — aluminum crochet hook No. 5

Measure and cut cardboard the same length as desired for fringe.

Wrap yarn around and around cardboard and cut along ONE EDGE ONLY. 214

Taking 3 or 4 pieces of yarn, match ends of yarn and fold to meet the "shortest" piece of yarn. 215

Using crochet hook, insert through edge of piece, being sure to go in at least two threads on edge, place hook through fold of yarn, pull through piece, place hook under all ends of fringe and pull yarn through loop. 216

Pull up into knot to fit piece. Trim ends. 217

KNIT TIP: You may use as many thicknesses of yarn as desired. You may use any length desired. The more thickness of yarn the greater distance there should be between the fringe knots.

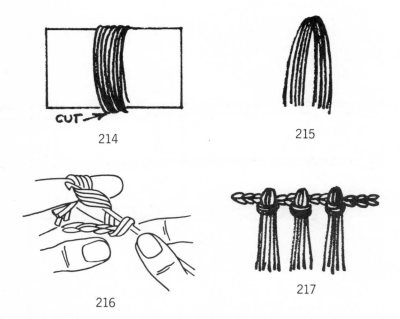

214

215

216

217

TASSLE

Measure and cut cardboard the length desired for tassel.

Place double yarn at top of card for tying.

Wrap yarn up and down around cardboard until thickness desired. 218

With tie, make one loop to hold tassel together. Remove cardboar. Pull tie tight and make several knots. Leave ends for fastening. 219

Take another piece of yarn and wrap around tassel several times about 1" from top. Run tying ends through top of tassel to hide fastenings. 220

Trim bottom of tassel and fasten on. 221

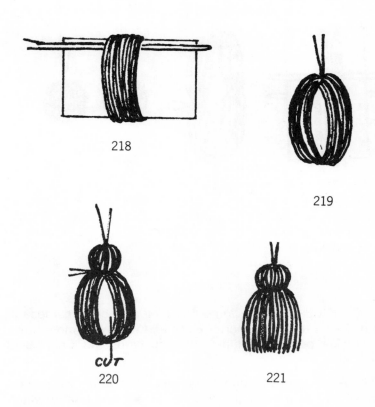

218

219

220

221

HOW TO MAKE POM PONS
(Two at one time)

Cut piece of heavy cardboard the height of TWO pom pons. Cut two pieces of yarn to tie with. Double these pieces and place one across center front and one across center back of cardboard.

Wrap yarn up and down around cardboard, wrapping in layers so yarn will not be in one spot only. 222

Tie each side with one loop so yarn will not slip out of place. Remove cardboard. Pull tying ends very tightly and make several knots. Repeat on other side. Holding tied places together, cut through yarn at top and bottom. 223

Shake out and trim pom pons into shape. Tie onto garments. 224

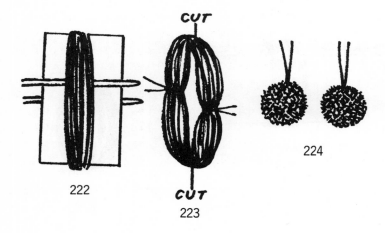

222

223

224

KNIT TIP: It is very easy to get too long a piece of cardboard. It would be better to have a shorter piece and wrap yarn more times to make thicker pom pons. I usually wrap cardboard from 60 to 100 times.

NOTE: There are commercial pom pon makers on the market which make one at a time and another (a wooden frame) which makes 8 at one time.

HOW TO MAKE CORD 225

Measure off 4 times the finished length cord desired. Matching ends, fold one time.

Have another person hold one end and stretching yarn until tight, twist yarn between thumb and fingers until very tightly twisted. Place finger in center of yarn and keeping yarn tight, place ends together. Release center section and yarn will twist into a cord.

Make a knot at end of loose yarn. Trim end.

KNIT TIP: If cord is not tight enough, yarn was not twisted enough. If cord is too thin, use more thickness of yarn. This can be redone easily.

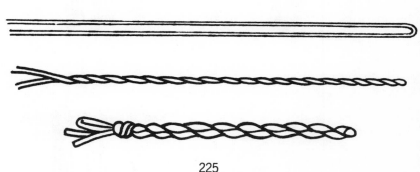

225

ADVICE FROM AND ADVICE TO KNITTERS

Should you listen and do what other knitters tell you because they have knitted longer than you? Have had more experience than you?

Always LISTEN to ideas or hints from other knitters. Unfortunately, bad habits and ideas, as well as good habits and ideas, are passed along from knitter to knitter, since most of us have learned from each other and few have had access to professional instructions.

YOU must decide how much you wish to use of what you hear.

Beware of the knitters who think they "know everything". They can be spotted instantly because they will say, "Oh, yes, I know that. I've been knitting for years and years!" I find these knitters have closed their minds to everything and believe there is nothing more they can learn. These knitters are quite often embarrassed to find there is much to be learned.

Even if a knitter is so opinionated as to say, "Well, I always do it this way!", you may learn a little knit tip that can be useful in making your knitting easier, lovelier and even more practical. It just might solve a knitting problem that has been "bugging" you.

But DO have a mind of your own! LISTEN, but don't change successful knitting because someone comes along and insists that you do it her way. You knit what you want to! Try what you want! You can't hurt anything since you can always unravel the yarn and knit it again!

The person, regardless of ability, who will be most helpful to you will say, "You might try it this way.", "Here's another way.", "I've found this works for me.", "I've been doing the shaping like this so it will look better.", or, "This may not be correct but it works." This kind of knitter will be interested in your problems, offer her suggestions but not insist that you do it her way. She will probably admit she doesn't know all about knitting. I would be the first to say, I don't know all about knitting. NO ONE knows all about knitting.

Although some knitters may think this manual too detailed, elemental or possibly repetitious, all instructions and knit tips presented have been used as answers to questions by knitters, have been some ideas worked out to solve their problems and improve their knitting, and have made many successful knitters.

Good knitters love knitting. Good knitters are willing to learn and are constantly striving to improve their handiwork. They will listen, judge, and perhaps make some changes in their knitting habits. The art of handknitting will then bring you real pleasure and great pride in creating beautiful knits.

I know that you, too, have become a fine knitter THE RIGHT WAY.

Knittingly yours,

Evelyn Stiles Stewart

ITEM MADE	NAME OF YARN AND COMPANY	COLOR AND DYE LOT	NUMBER OF SKEINS OR BALLS	NEEDLE SIZES	GAUGE

Pattern on Page 64

Pattern on Page 69

Pattern on Page 64

Pattern on Page 68

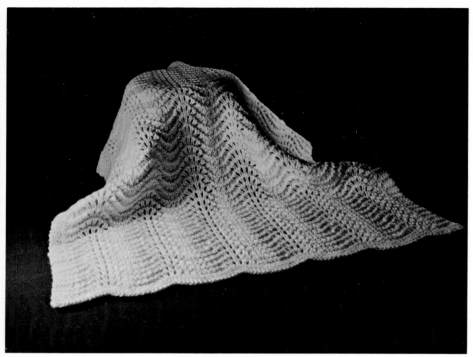

Pattern on Page 69

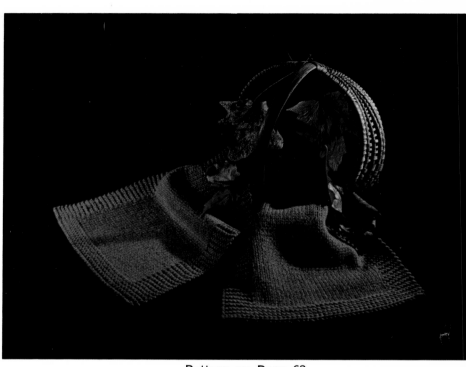

Pattern on Page 63

Pattern on Page 67

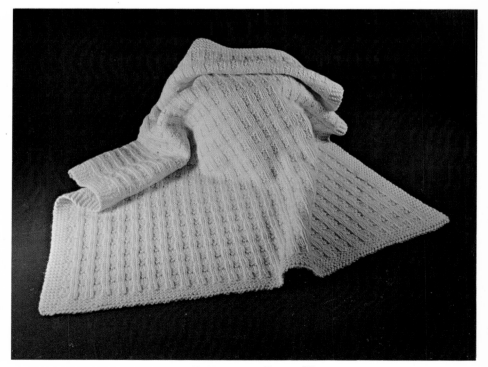

Pattern on Page 67

Pattern on Page 72

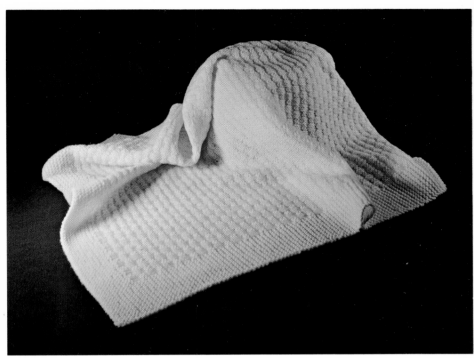

Pattern on Page 67

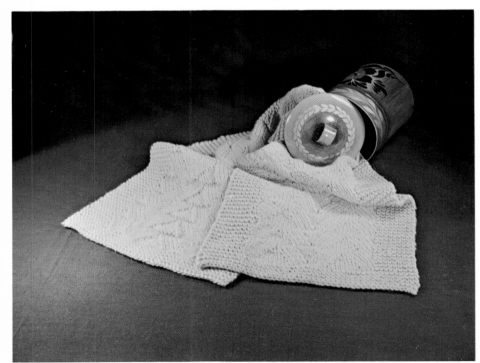

Pattern on Page 65

Patterns on Pages 66-70-71-72

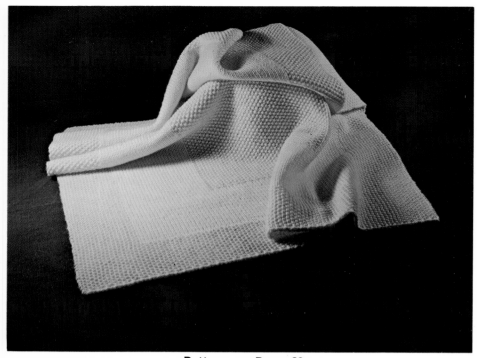

Pattern on Page 68

Pattern on Page 64

Pattern on Page 63

Pattern on Page 69